One Hundred and Fifty

Life Lessons

from Noble Narrations

Derived from the classes of
Ayatullah Nasir Makarim Shirazi
Translated by Seyed Ali Musawi

AL-KISA
FOUNDATION
UNDER THE CLOAK OF GUIDANCE AND MERCY

Photo credits: freepik.com, pixabay.com, unsplash.com, imamhussain.org, Hassan Roholamin (shiaarts.ir), deviantart.com.
Layout and Design by Irum Abbas.

Disclaimer: Religious texts have *not* been translated verbatim so as to meet the developmental and comprehension needs of the readers.

Library of Congress Control Number: 2022920593

For permission requests, please write to the publisher at the address below.

Kisa Publications
4415 Fortran Court
San Jose, CA 95134
info@alkisafoundation.org
alkisafoundation.org

DEDICATION

This book is dedicated to the beloved Imām of our time ﷻ. May Allah ﷻ hasten his reappearance and help us to become his true companions.

ACKNOWLEDGMENTS

"On the Day of Resurrection, the ink of the scholars will be weighed up against the blood of the martyrs, and the ink of the scholars will be heavier than the blood of the martyrs."

—NAHJ AL-FAṢĀḤAH, SAYING 3222

True reward lies with Allah ﷻ, but we would like to sincerely thank Sheikh Ehsan Ahmadi, and Sisters: Abeda Khimji, Arifa Hudda, Fatima Hussain, Irum Abbas, Naadirah Muhibullah, Qudsiyah Remtulla, Rumina Hashmani, Sabika Mithani, and Tasneem Hudda. We would especially like to acknowledge Seyed Ali Musawi - the translator of the original book written by Āyatullāh Nasir Makarim Shirazi.

May Allah ﷻ bless them in this world and the next.

Please Note: Some minor edits have been made to the original English translations where it was necessary.

MARḤŪMĪN DEDICATION

Please recite a Sūrah al-Fātiḥah for Marḥūmah Sugra Tajwala, daughter of Hassan Ali Wazir Chowdhury.

Preface

Prophet Muḥammad ﷺ has said: *"Nurture and raise your children in the best way. Raise them with the love of the Prophets ﷺ and the Ahl al-Bayt ؏."*

Literature and books are an influential form of media that often shapes the thoughts and views of an entire generation. Therefore, in order to establish an Islamic foundation for the future generations, there is a dire need for compelling Islamic literature. Over the past several years, this need has become increasingly prevalent throughout Islamic centers and schools everywhere. Due to the growing dissonance between parents, children, society, and the teachings of Islam and the Ahl al-Bayt ؏, this need has become even more pressing. Al-Kisa Foundation, along with its subsidiary, Kisa Kids Publications, was established in an effort to help bridge this gap with the guidance of scholars (*'ulamā'*) and the help of educators. We would like to make this a communal effort and platform. Therefore, we sincerely welcome constructive feedback and help in any capacity.

The goal of this book, *150 Life Lessons from Noble Narrations*, is to encourage readers to connect with the wealth of traditions *(ḥadīth)* that we have from our immaculate role models - Prophet Muḥammad ﷺ and his Ahl al-Bayt ؏, as a famous *ḥadīth* says: *"Anyone who memorizes and preserves 40 traditions (ḥadīth) will certainly reach a great status."*[1]

These 150 narrations *(ḥadīth)* contained in this book were taught by the renowned Āyatullāh Nasir Makarim Shirazi in his Ethics and Morals *(Akhlāq)* classes, and were later compiled into a book. Āyatullāh Makarim is indeed an esteemed scholar who has dedicated his entire life in the service of Islam, especially to create meaningful resources for our future generations. Likewise, the translator, Seyed Ali Musawi, is a scholar based in the USA, and has authored and translated many books in an effort for content to reach, and inshā'Allāh, resonate with the audience today and always.

Narrations *(ḥadīth)* are an ocean of knowledge, and in this book we share some direct points that a person can take as a foundation for implementing these life lessons, and apply them to one's practical life, with the understanding that for sure there are different angles and more depth in each *ḥadīth* to explore.

It is important to note that although the *ḥadīth* have been compiled from reputable books, and are used in many classes by great scholars, including Āyatullāh Makarim, the exact page number, etc. of the *ḥadīth* may differ based on various editions of the original books. Likewise, some of the sources may be incomplete. Also, the *ḥadīth* have not always translated verbatim, rather some of them have been paraphrased in order to understand them better.

We hope that you and your families enjoy this book, and that it becomes a means to plant the love and connection of Prophet Muḥammad ﷺ and his Ahl al-Bayt ؏, inshā'Allāh.

We pray to Allah ﷻ to give us the strength and ability *(tawfīq)* to perform our duties and responsibilities.

With Du'ās,
Nabi R. Mir (Abidi)

[1] *Mīzān al-Ḥikmah*, Ḥadīth 4246.

Introduction

by Āyatullāh Nasir Makarim Shirazi

In the Name of Allah, the All-Beneficent, the All-Merciful

Our greatest treasures of knowledge after the Noble Qur'ān are the practices of Prophet Muḥammad ﷺ and the valuable traditions *(ḥadīth)* of the Household of the Prophet ﷺ.

Unfortunately, these traditions - which are without any dispute - oceans of science and knowledge are yet to be known and understood. There are many traditions that in one short phrase speak volumes in terms of useful lessons which can solve many problems that we are facing today as a society on a whole. This book is a selection of such powerful and meaningful traditions - together with translations and brief descriptions for each narration.

It all started with the Friday weekly interpretation discussion meetings at the Assembly of Religion and Science inside the Imām al-Ḥusayn Masjid in Tehran. A tradition was selected, and everyone was to practice it throughout the week as a lesson. The traditions were so well received that it was decided to publish them.

This small book serves as an example of Islam's richness for those who want to know more about this religion better through a short study. What is even more important in appreciating their worth is the practicing of these programs in our lives. Let us pray to Allah for success in understanding these narrations, and then being able to act upon them.

Nasir Makarim Shirazi
Qum, 1976
The Month of Shawwāl, 1397 AH

Symbol Usage

Throughout this work, when taking the name of any of the revered personalities in Islamic history, including Allah, Prophet Muḥammad, his select family members, and religious scholars, we have employed the following Arabic symbols to show the reverence to each of them. As a part of Islamic culture, readers are requested to send the salutations upon these personalities when they read this work.

سبحانه وتعالى	*All glory belongs to God, the Glorified and Exalted* Used exclusively for God (Allah)
صلى الله عليه وآله وسلم	*Blessings of Allah be upon him and his Immaculate Progeny* Used exclusively for Prophet Muḥammad
عليه السلام	*Peace be upon him* Used for one honored male
عليهم السلام	*Peace be upon all of them* Used for three or more honored men or women or a combination
عليها السلام	*Peace be upon her* Used for one honored female
عجّل الله تعالى فرجه الشريف	*May Allah, the Most High, hasten his noble return* Used exclusively for Imām al-Mahdī

Transliteration Chart

Arabic terms in this book have been transliterated according to the following guidelines*:

ء	a, i, or u (initial form)	ص	ṣ
ء	’(medial or final form)	ض	ḍ
ا	a	ط	ṭ
ب	b	ظ	ẓ
ت	t	ع	‘
ث	th	غ	gh
ج	j	ف	f
ح	ḥ	ق	q
خ	kh	ك	k
د	d	ل	l
ذ	dh	م	m
ر	r	ن	n
ز	z	ه	h
س	s	و	w
ش	sh	ي	y

ـَ	a	آ / ـَا / ىٰ	ā
ـِ	i	ـِي	ī
ـُ	u	ـُو	ū
ـّ	double letter		

*Please note that due to limitations, the transliteration is not 100% accurate in capturing tajwīd rules.

Contents

n
r
r∥
r⊥
v = v∥ + v⊥
v∥ = k(k·v)
v⊥ = − k×(k×v) = v − k(k·v)
x
y
(x',y')
(x,y)
E

LESSON ONE

Thought, Contemplation, and Reflection

It has been said by the Maʿṣūmīn ﷺ:

Know that there is no benefit in knowledge without thought.

Know that there is no benefit in the recitation of the Qurʾān without contemplation.

Know that worship without reflection is without effect.[1]

Filling the mind with various sorts of scientific formulas, logical precepts, philosophical principles, and other types of knowledge is of extremely little value unless it is accompanied with proper thinking. If a person simply memorizes facts without considering their greater meaning, then this will be of no benefit for them.

When a person simply recites the Noble Qurʾān there are benefits and rewards to this; however, one will not receive the full effects of the guidance that Allah ﷻ sent it down for unless it is accompanied by contemplation and reflection into the depths of the meanings which are found within the verses.

Finally, worship without reflection is like physical movement with no real purpose, and it lacks the loftier effects that such worship can have on the human soul.

[1] *Uṣūl al-Kāfī*, Vol. 1, P. 36; *Tuḥaf al-ʿUqūl.*

LESSON TWO

The Measure of Reflection

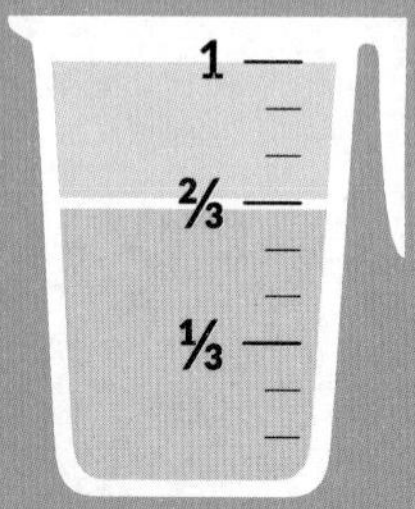

Imām aṣ-Ṣādiq has said:

The reformation of life is completed through a measure that is two-thirds caution and one-third a lack of care and attention.[2]

Nothing can ever be completed without careful study, planning, and caution. At the same time, nothing can ever be completed without a lack of care either. How can this be since these two statements appear to be a complete contradiction?

[2] *Tuḥaf al-'Uqūl*, P. 267.

The answer to this is that if we want to do something without studying about it, proper planning, and attention, then we will not be able to take that to completion. At the same time, if we want to plan for all of the possible things that could happen or all of the things that could go wrong, then we would become bogged down with so many possibilities, that even simple tasks would end up taking years upon years of difficult planning and thought.

In a nutshell, over thinking and over planning play a role similar to a lack of thought and proper planning. A person needs to have these two elements in the proper proportions in order to achieve one's goals.

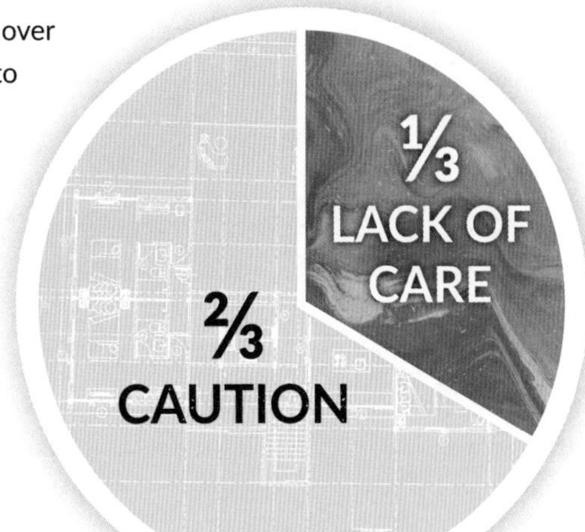

They Pay so Much Attention to the Food They Eat, But...

Imām Ḥasan al-Mujtabā ﷺ has said:

I am surprised at those who reflect on the food that they eat, but they do not think at all about the food of their soul. They stay away from unhealthy foods, but they fill their heart with various destructive matters.[3]

Just as the Imām ﷺ has mentioned, people are very careful in regards to what they eat. They will only eat foods that they trust, and if there is even a 10% chance of catching an illness or food poisoning, they will not even think about eating that food. Some people go beyond this and follow all sorts of nutritional rules that they believe will improve their health. In a nutshell, people care deeply about the foods they eat (and this is very good and beneficial to do).

[3] *Safīnat al-Biḥār*, Section on Food.

However, when it comes to the food pertaining to their soul, they take in whatever they find, regardless of how it will affect them. Even if they are about to take in something that has a 95% chance of giving them an illness or spiritual poisoning, they really do not pay any attention to the danger. If people slander or backbite others in their presence, they sit and listen without any concern. This is, in reality, the equivalent of eating a plate of completely rotten and spoiled food; it is going to make them extremely ill, even though they may not realize it right away.

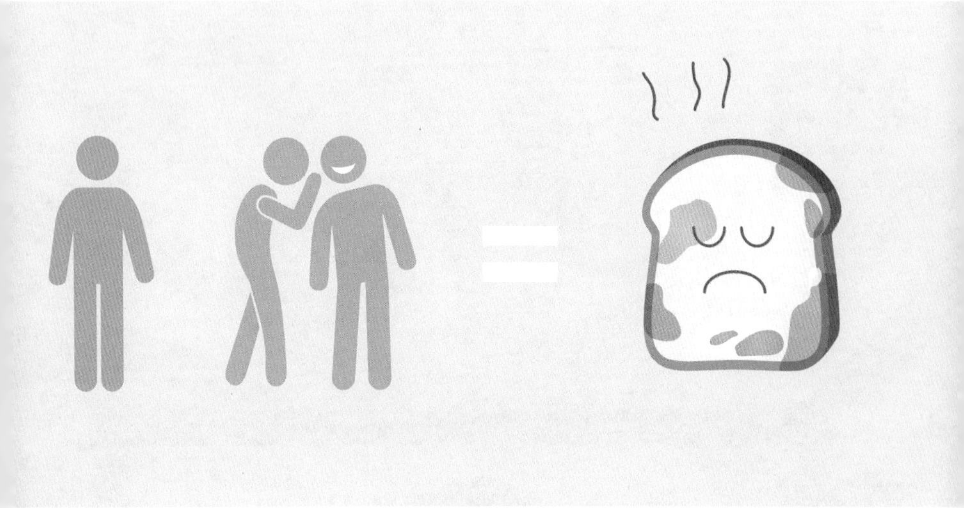

What we must understand is that various things which relate to the soul will naturally have an effect on it, and the soul grows or diminishes as a result of what we take in. This is exactly like when we eat food and our bodies either grow strong from it, or become ill as a result of it. It is truly amazing that people pay such detailed attention to the food related to their physical bodies, but are so utterly careless and oblivious when it comes to the food of their souls.

The Role of the Pen

Imām aṣ-Ṣādiq ﷺ has said:

I have not seen anything weeping as beautifully as a pen when it smiles.[4]

The pen is an amazing means of expression of the various human emotions and points of wisdom. It can be said that the pen is what gave rise to the concept of civilization, and it is what allows society to function in such a smooth fashion. The pen expresses the pain that people feel, and it also expresses the vitality and life that is within them. This medium expresses love, excitement, sorrow, and the very beauty of life.

At the same time, if this pen falls into the hands of unworthy individuals, then it weeps blood rather than ink, and its smile transforms into a cruel smirk, which will eventually remove the highest of human values and morals.

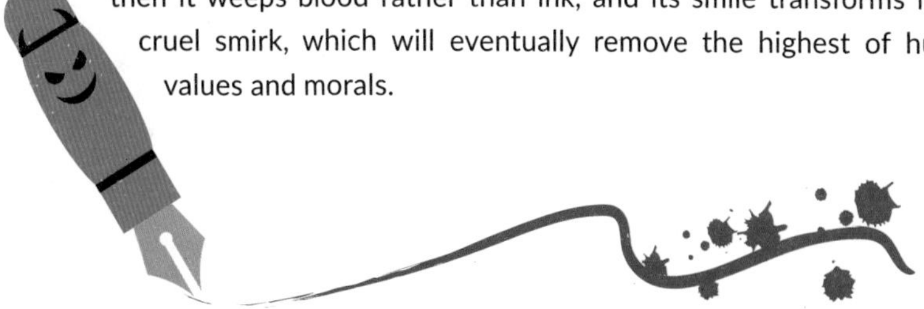

[4] *Laṭāʾif wa Ẓarāʾif.*

In Between Two Great Responsibilities

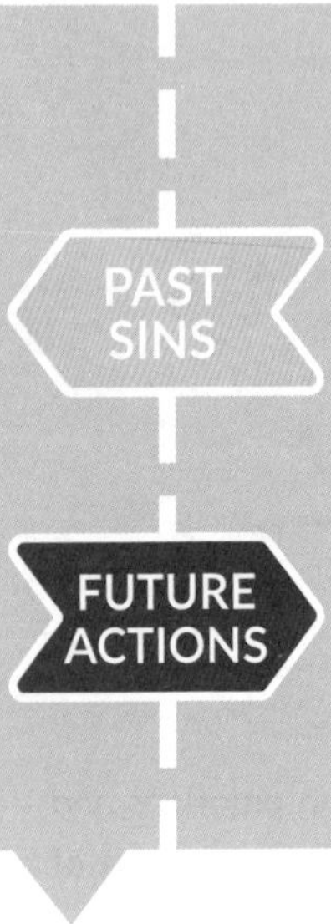

Imām aṣ-Ṣādiq has said:

A faithful person is always worried about two things. The first includes the past sins for which one does not know how Allah will act in regards to them; and the second is about what is left of one's life, during which an individual is uncertain about how one will behave.[5]

The clearest sign of faith is a sense of responsibility toward one's own actions, as well as the duties by which one must abide. Someone who acknowledges these two responsibilities will always be thinking about ways to fulfill them, as well as making up for past lapses. Such a person will always consider how they can best act in regards to their duties and make the most productive use of the time that they have left in this temporary world.

[5] *Uṣūl al-Kāfī*, Vol. 2, P. 7.

LESSON SIX

Factors that Lead Toward Societal Destruction

It has been said by the Maʿṣūmīn ﷺ:

There are four things in a home which, even if one of them is present, will cause the blessings of Allah ﷻ to be removed and result in its utter destruction. These are treachery, theft, the consumption of alcohol, and adultery (actions performed which go against chastity).[6]

These four things not only apply to a home, but also relate to society at large. For example, when treachery becomes commonplace and permeates through society, then the spirit of trust will leave it. When theft becomes common, then society will be robbed of peace and security. When the use of alcohol becomes rampant, then people will not think properly, children will be born with various problems, and the youth will not utilize their time and energy in the best manner. When society becomes affected by adultery or a lack of chastity, then the foundation of the family will be shaken, and future generations will be pulled toward corruption.

[6] *Nahj al-Faṣāḥah.*

LESSON SEVEN

Laziness and Poverty

Imām ʿAlī has said:

On the day when all things were paired together, laziness and weakness were joined to one another and this gave birth to poverty.[7]

Everything is gained through hard work and struggle. This is a reality that Islam has taught us. Laziness, a lack of desire, and escape from the hardships and difficulties that one faces in life is not in concordance with faith. These are things that will bring about not only financial poverty, but also poverty in one's morals and spiritual state. People of faith should try their utmost to be independent in all aspects and not rely on others for assistance.

[7] *Biḥār al-Anwār*, Vol. 78; P. 59; *Tuḥaf al-ʿUqūl*, P. 158.

These are things that will bring about not just financial poverty, but also poverty in one's morals and spiritual state.

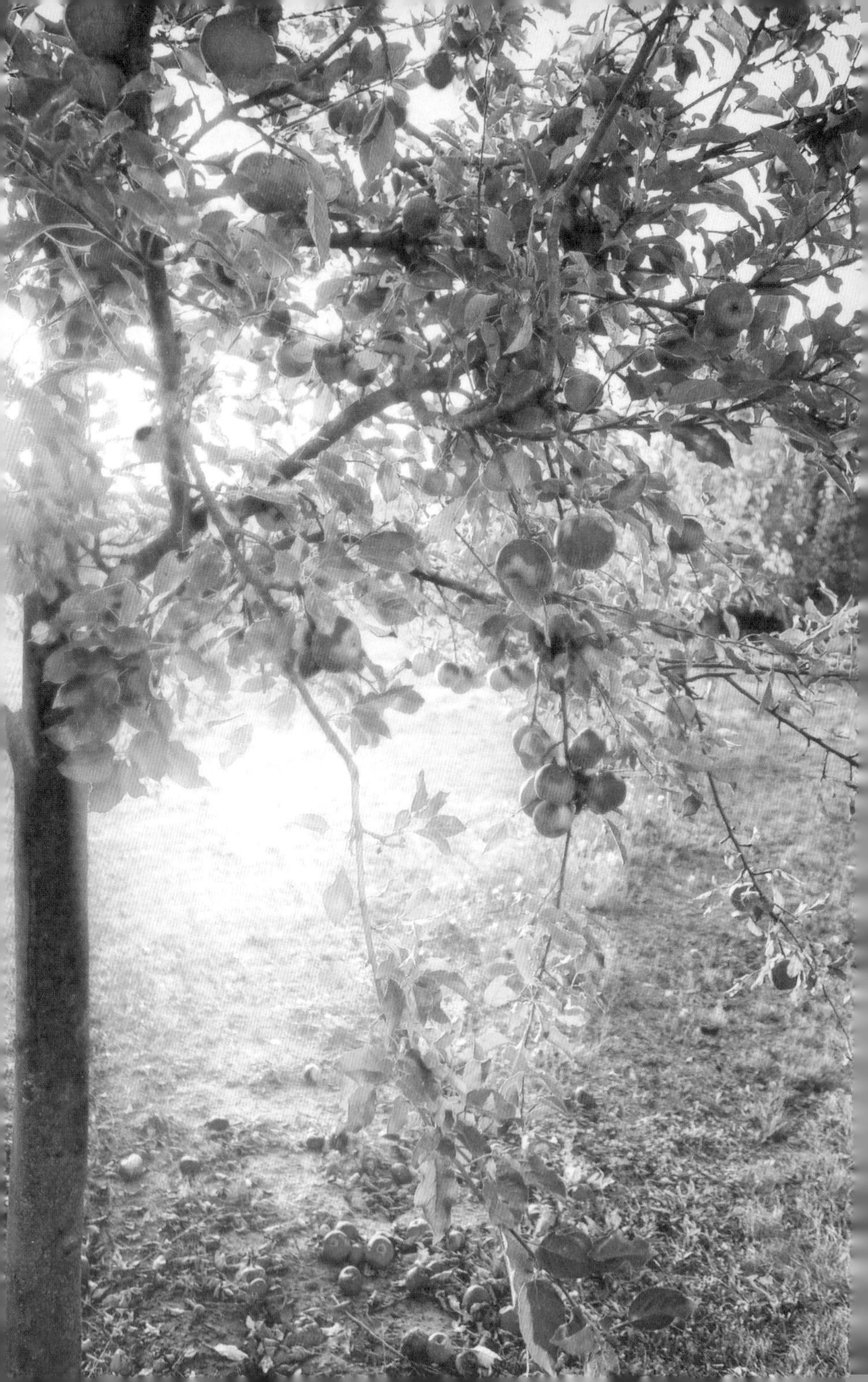

Descent of Knowledge upon the Hearts

Luqmān, the famous sage, has said:

O my son, Allah ﷻ enlivens the hearts of people through the light of knowledge and understanding, just like the dead earth is brought to life with the rain that descends from the skies.[8]

The heart is like a fertile orchard that has various trees and plants growing within it. It possesses different herbs, fruit-bearing trees, and flowers. If these plants are watered and taken care of in the proper way, then all of the plants will reach their full potential and beauty. The means through which this orchard can be watered is through the rain of knowledge and understanding. It is for this same reason that the hearts of those without knowledge are completely barren and dead, unable to give fruit or anything else of value. In all situations, we must strive to enliven ourselves with the light of knowledge and understanding.

[8] *Biḥār al-Anwār*, Vol. 1.

The Root of Arrogance

Imām aṣ-Ṣādiq ﷺ has said:

There is no person who acts arrogantly toward others except due to a weakness that one senses within oneself.[9]

Today, it has been proven through psychological studies that arrogance and proud behavior can be the result of a feeling of inferiority that people possess within themselves. People who suffer from this inferiority complex try to use this misguided technique to appear superior to others. Yet, this type of behavior only adds to their inferiority because people recognize them for who they truly are. Over time, this kind of behavior will increase others' hate and disgust for them. This psychological issue was mentioned over a thousand years ago by Imām aṣ-Ṣādiq ﷺ. On the other hand, people who have faith are inspired by a particular inner state, which inclines them toward modesty and humility.

[9] *Biḥār al-Anwār*, Vol. 73, P. 225.

LESSON TEN

Three Valuable Sounds in the View of Allah ﷻ

Prophet Muḥammad ﷺ has said:

There are three sounds which will penetrate through the veils and reach the presence of Allah ﷻ, the Almighty: the sound of a scholar's pen as they begin to write, the sound of the footsteps of the warriors (mujāhidīn) on the battlefield, and the sound of a weaving machine by chaste women. [10]

There are three sounds that extend to the very source of creation and continue on for eternity. The first of these sounds is that of a pen, even though it virtually has no sound. The second is the sound of the footsteps of warriors as they maneuver toward the enemy in defending themselves and their society. The third is the sound of hard work and struggle, such as a woman sewing, even if it may seem to be very simple at first glance. A harmonious society is composed of these three important elements: knowledge, struggle against the enemies, and hard work and effort.

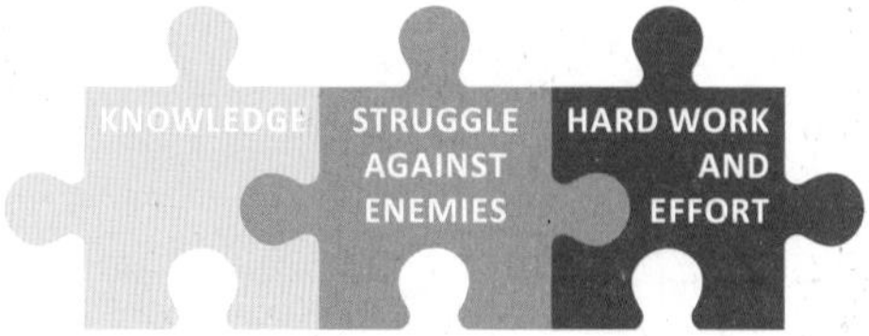

[10] *Ashshahāb fī al-Ḥikam wal-Ādāb*, P. 22.

Photo: imamhussain.org

The Martyrdom of Imām Ḥusayn عليه السلام

Prophet Muḥammad ﷺ has said:

The martyrdom of Imām Ḥusayn عليه السلام creates a fire and heat in the hearts of the believers that can never be extinguished.[11]

There have been many different wars throughout history that have been all but forgotten just a few months or years after they ended. Yet, if someone fights in the way of Allah ﷻ and struggles in the path of liberating one's fellow human beings, then this is something that will never be forgotten. This is because fighting for the sake of Allah ﷻ, as well as for concepts such as freedom, honor, and dignity, are timeless and will never be forgotten. Imām Ḥusayn عليه السلام and his companions fought for these very values, and it is for this reason that their memory will live on forever.

[11] *Mustadrak al-Wasāʾil*, Vol. 2, P. 217.

Two Signs of a True Muslim

Prophet Muḥammad ﷺ has said:

Do not look only at the abundance of prayers, fasting, Ḥajj pilgrimages, night vigils, or good acts (toward others) of the people (even though these things are important). Rather, look at their truthfulness and trustworthiness.[12]

When a person looks at the Islamic traditions, it becomes clear that there are two definite signs of a true Muslim: truthfulness and trustworthiness. Even though acts of worship such as prayers, fasting, and Ḥajj are all very important and instrumental in the growth of human beings, these should not be considered the only signs of faith. They must be accompanied with the attributes of truthfulness and trustworthiness.

[12] *Safīnat al-Biḥār.*

The Fire of Anger

Imām al-Bāqir ﷺ has said:

Anger and rage are burning flames from Shayṭān, which are lit in the innermost sections of the heart of an individual.[13]

It is extremely rare for someone to perform an action while in a state of anger and rage and not be regretful about its consequences later on. This is because these emotions cause the intellect and the process of correct decision making to completely fall by the wayside. In fact, the entire human system is so affected by anger and rage that in certain cases, people end up doing things that they regret for the rest of their lives. When a person becomes angry, they must quickly contain their anger and work to extinguish it as soon as possible with the virtue of patience (ṣabr). If they do not do this, then the fire of this rage may consume both themselves, as well as those around them.

[13] *Biḥār al-Anwār*, Vol. 73, P. 278.

The Sources of Wealth

Prophet Muḥammad ﷺ has said:

Seek your sustenance in the hidden places of the earth.[14]

During a time when the concept behind mining for minerals was not very common, the Prophet ﷺ instructed the Muslims that if they wished to seek their sustenance, they should look within the depths of the earth.

Such instructions show both the wisdom of Islamic teachings, as well as the importance of struggling in the way of gaining a lawful and honorable sustenance.

[14] *Nahj al-Faṣāḥah*, Fuqh al-Qur'ān, Vol. 2, P. 22.

The Worst of Professions

Prophet Muḥammad ﷺ has said:

The worst wealth that one can gain is that of usury (ribā).[15]

Imām aṣ-Ṣādiq (a) has said:

Whenever Allah ﷻ wishes to destroy a nation, usury becomes conspicuous amongst them.[16]

In spite of the widespread prevalence of usury in our world today, and the seemingly addictive dependence of the world economy upon it, there is no question that usury, as a system, ends up destroying the society in which it is allowed to exist.

Usury causes wealth to accumulate in an unnatural way in the hands of a few individuals, and this unjust distribution of wealth is the root of various societal and ethical ills.

[15] *Wasāʾil ash-Shīʿah*, Vol. 18, P. 122; *Biḥār al-Anwār*, Vol. 21, P. 210

[16] *Wasāʾil ash-Shīʿah*, Vol. 12, Pp. 426-427; *Wasāʾil ash-Shīʿah*, Vol. 18, P. 123.

Rulership and Slavery

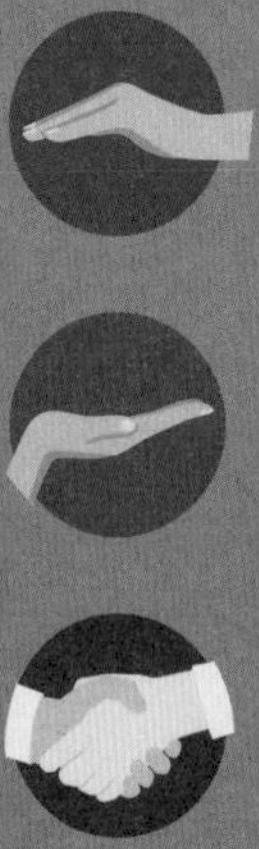

Imām ʿAlī ﷺ has said:

Do good toward whomever you like, and you will rule over them;

Be dependent on whomever you like, and you will become their slave;

And be self-sufficient over whomever you like, and you will become equal to them.[17]

When it comes to the social interactions of people, this is a rule that holds completely true in regards to their relationships with one another. Those who consistently give are always at an advantage, while those who consistently receive are always at a disadvantage. This also applies to nations, for if a nation is one that primarily receives from others, then it will eventually be treated like an inferior slave. Those nations who give to others will be treated like masters and leaders of those who receive. A true Muslim is one who establishes a social relationship with others based on both giving and receiving, not simply based on one of these aspects. Those who receive aid should be those who are disabled and truly unable to work or provide for themselves.

[17] *Al-Khīsāl*, Vol. 2, P. 420; *Biḥār al-Anwār*, Vol. 74, P. 400; *Rowzat al-Wāʿeẓīn*, Vol. 1, P. 109.

LESSON SEVENTEEN

Religious Falsity and Posturing

Imām aṣ-Ṣādiq (a) has said:

Do not perform good actions for the sake of posturing or showing off to people who neither have the power of life or death, nor the power of solving any problems for you.[18]

Those who become used to showing off and posturing in front of others end up living lives that are completely empty and devoid of any substance. Due to this manner of living, their lives begin to lack all felicity and happiness. They only possess the very outer aspects of religion and religiosity, and they suffice with dry rituals when it comes to their religious practices. It is for this same reason that Islam has severely criticized this type of behavior. Since the people they are trying to impress have no power over one's destiny, why should they behave in such a way? Such a thing is not only illogical, but it is also of no benefit to anyone.

[18] *Biḥār al-Anwār*, Vol. 72, P. 300.

LESSON EIGHTEEN

Jealousy

Imām aṣ-Ṣādiq ﷺ has said:

A jealous person will end up harming oneself before harming the object of one's jealousy.[19]

Jealousy is a state in which one cannot bear to see others enjoying certain blessings. As a result, such an individual may even go as far as trying to take away that blessing from the other person, and if they end up failing, then they may attempt to hurt that person in other ways.

In reality, a jealous person is always trying to take things away from others, instead of trying to push oneself toward reaching a higher level.

There is no doubt that jealousy is a serious moral disease with intense social and spiritual consequences. From the perspective of psychological and spiritual well-being, a jealous person will end up harming oneself to a greater extent than the individual whom they are jealous of.

[19] *Biḥār al-Anwār*, Vol. 73, P. 225.

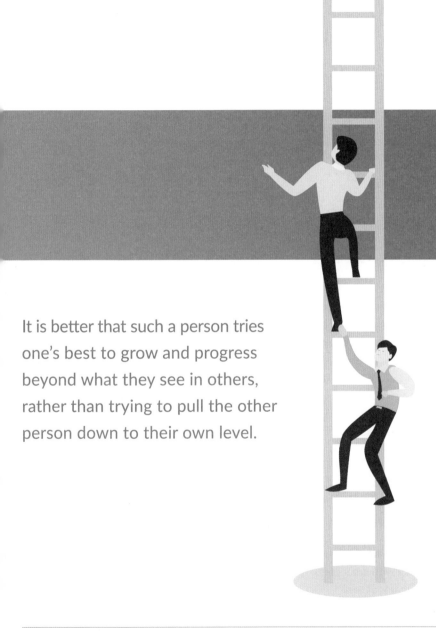

It is better that such a person tries one's best to grow and progress beyond what they see in others, rather than trying to pull the other person down to their own level.

The Ones Who are Far from Allah's Mercy

Imām ʿAlī has said:

One who has land and water available to them, and is still poor and needy in spite of this, is truly far from the mercy of Allah.[20]

From the Islamic source books, it is clear that Muslims are duty bound to put to use all of the resources they have at their disposal in a responsible and conscientious way. This includes resources such as animal husbandry, farming, mining of underground resources, the establishment of factories, trade, etc. One of the teachings of Islam is to make the full utilization of the resources that we have been blessed with. If we make a habit of using these resources with 100% efficiency, then this will cause our worldly life to be full of blessings and prosperity; and the rewards of these actions will also spread to other aspects of our lives.

If we can incorporate working hard and being successful with the resources that Allah has blessed us with, then this will extend into our spiritual and religious life as well.

As a result, we will find that our religious life will be filled with great blessings and closeness to our Creator as well.

[20] *Biḥār al-Anwār*, Vol. 103, P. 65.

The Worst Friends

Imām ʿAlī ﷺ has said:

Your worst friends are those who flatter and praise you, but hide your defects from you.[21]

Fleeing from reality and covering the truth will never help us resolve the various issues that we face in our day-to-day lives. It is for this same reason that when our friends hide from us the realities they see within us, rather than helping us through constructive criticism, they are doing us the greatest disservice. Usually, this is done in order to gain the favor of a friend, or it is seen as a positive attribute where one only mentions the good things about a friend and hides all of the negatives. However, the truth is that such actions are actually being disloyal to one's friends, even if they do not recognize it as such. In some cases, this kind of harmful behavior can end up costing these friends dearly later on in life.

[21] *Ghurar al-Ḥikam,* Section on: The Brother, the Friend, the Associate, and the Companion, Ḥadīth 78.

The Completion of One's Actions

Prophet Muḥammad ﷺ has said:

Completing and following through with good actions is better and more important than simply initiating them.[22]

In our social or religious lives, we often begin performing good actions with great zeal and eagerness. Yet, as time passes, we sometimes lose focus and leave the work unfinished. Islam encourages people to work hard and develop a level of determination such that when they begin various good actions, they push through and take them to completion. We should have a greater focus on trying to finish what we start rather than simply beginning new things and then not completing them.

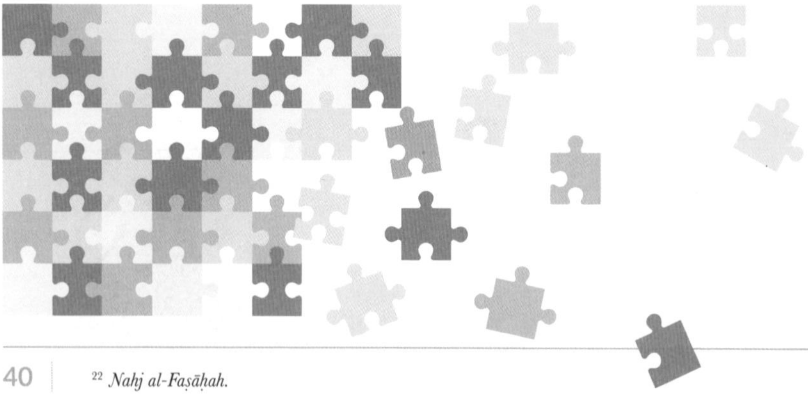

[22] *Nahj al-Faṣāḥah.*

Everlasting Plans

Imām aṣ-Ṣādiq has said:

Allah ordered all of His Prophets to invite the people of the world to truthfulness and the giving back of trusts.[23]

A healthy society must possess certain foundations, and the most important of these is that of public trust. This includes trusts related to speech, as well action. Naturally, the biggest enemy of these two things is lying and treachery. If we look at a society where lying and treachery has become commonplace, we find that people fear one another and bear their burdens alone, and are thus isolated and disconnected. It is for this reason that inviting people to truthfulness and safeguarding what people have entrusted are two of the most foundational aspects of the Prophetic message that Allah sent down to humanity.

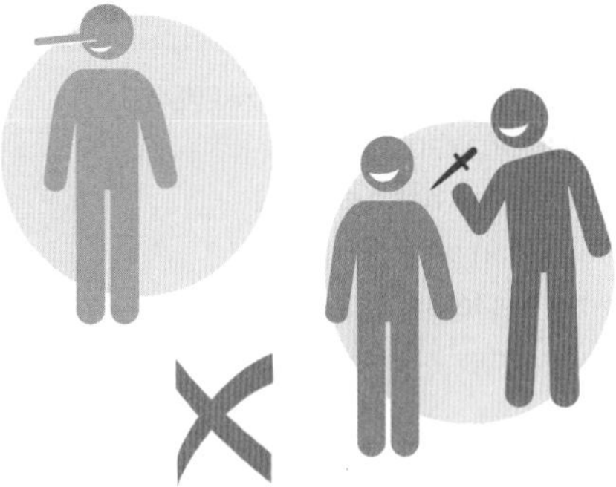

[23] *Safīnat al-Biḥār.*

The Severest of Punishments

Prophet Muḥammad ﷺ has said:

A person who knows something but does not act upon it or does not apply one's knowledge will be punished more severely than others on the Day of Judgment.[24]

From an Islamic perspective, knowledge is a tool used primarily for action. Through actively utilizing knowledge, a person can improve one's own life and the lives of those around them. Without the element of action, knowledge will be of no use for humanity. Those who lack knowledge are less culpable than those who know, but still choose to act improperly. When someone knows something but still acts contrary to one's knowledge, this is a heavy responsibility for which they will be asked about on the Day of Judgment. Everyone is responsible to the same degree as the level of one's knowledge. A person who has more knowledge has a greater duty than an individual who has less knowledge.

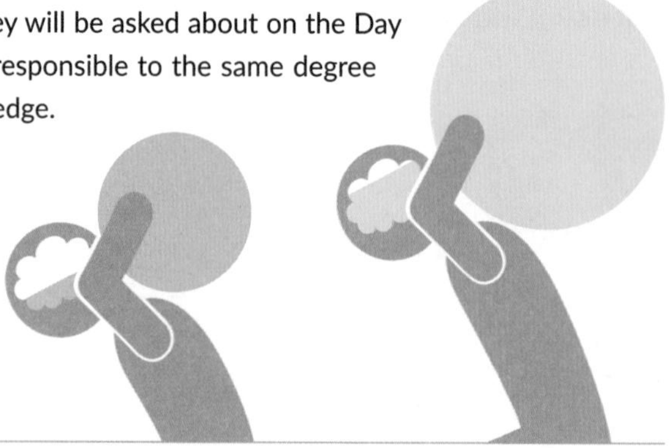

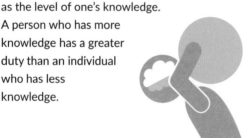

[24] *Biḥār al-Anwār*, Vol. 2, P. 38.

The Calamity of Debt

Prophet Muḥammad ﷺ has said:

Avoid taking loans as much as possible, for it brings sorrow during the nights and hopelessness during the days.[25]

The glitter of the modern-day lifestyle and never-ending race for amassing newer and better possessions has led a great number of people into the abyss of debt. Unfortunately, a lot of times this debt is without any real need or purpose, and it will cause great difficulties in their lives. Someone who is indebted is not really a free individual, and it is for this reason that Islam instructs us not to take loans unless there is a pressing need. What we have mentioned about individuals also applies to societies and nations. A nation should be wary of becoming indebted to others, for such debt can cause them to become slaves, and it can chip away at their independence and freedom.

[25] *Biḥār al-Anwār*, Vol. 103, P. 141.

A Healthy Social Life

Imām aṣ-Ṣādiq ﷺ has said:

If people honored the mutual rights of one another and helped those in need, their lives would become more pleasant and satisfying for them.[26]

The aforementioned tradition tells us that if we pay close attention to other people's rights and take care of the needy, then the quality of our lives will improve dramatically. This shows that the financial rights of people cannot be considered as just an ethical or moral issue. It is, in reality, an important foundational aspect of social life, which brings about widespread societal health and peace.

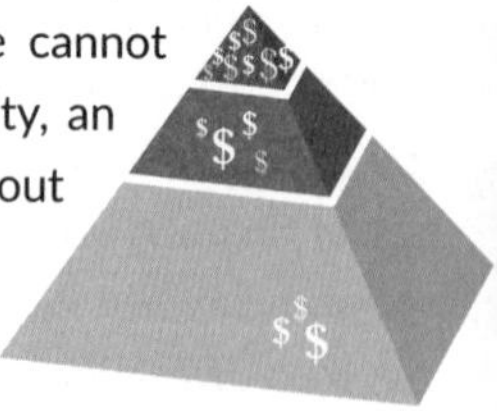

The dangerous situation that we have at hand today, where society has been divided into varying classes, shows how important this issue really is. As long as people in this world believe that 'might makes right,' this issue will never be resolved. Everyone needs to understand that just because someone is momentarily powerful, this does not allow them to usurp the rights of others. Eventually, the 'chickens will come home to roost,' and a great price will have to be paid.

[26] *Wasā'il ash-Shī'ah*, Vol. 6, P. 2.

The Key to Misfortune

Imām Ḥasan al-ʿAskarī has said:

Allah created a lock for all evils, and the key to this lock is found in wine (alcohol). Yet lying is even worse than alcohol.[27]

The greatest preventative tool against the evils found in this world is the faculty of the intellect. This is the most secure 'lock' that has been placed upon these evils. However, this 'lock' can easily be opened with the 'key' of alcohol, and once it has been opened, all of these evils will come rushing out. When a person is in a drunken state, they will say and do almost anything, and even the greatest of sins will not seem so evil anymore.

Even though a drunken person commits sins due to a lack of proper judgment, an individual who lies with full awareness will destroy the bonds upon which society has been established. When such trust is broken in the society, it will give rise to an unbelievable level of sin, deviation, and widespread corruption. It is for this reason that lying is considered to be even more dangerous than alcohol.

[27] *Wasāʾil ash-Shīʿah*, Vol. 2, P. 223.

Signs of those Bound for Heaven

Imām aṣ-Ṣādiq ﷺ has said:

The people of Paradise have four signs: a smiling and open face, an expressive tongue, a heart full of love and affection, and a generous and giving hand.[28]

The most authentic religion is one that recognizes human beings as the very heart of society, and causes that society to give rise to valuable individuals. This is because

the social sphere is the root of all spiritual and material blessings found on this earth.

The aforementioned tradition brings forward four signs of those who are bound for Heaven. It is interesting to note that all of these signs are related to socially relevant issues and are not of an individual worship-based nature.

The first sign is a relaxed and open face that is full of joy and affection. The second is a tongue which expresses love and speaks good words to the people in a clear and eloquent way. The third sign is a heart that feels emotions for other people, while the fourth is a hand that does not refrain from helping others. These are the signs of those who will be led to Paradise.

[28] *Irshād al-Qulūb.*

Signs of the Hypocrites

Imām aṣ-Ṣādiq ﷺ has said:

Luqmān said to his son: 'The hypocrites have three signs: their tongues are not in concordance with their hearts, their hearts are not in concordance with their actions, and their outer is not in concordance with their inner.'[29]

Hypocrisy is a dangerous disease which arises from a deficiency in one's personality and lack of willpower. People who attempt to show themselves as something they are not, and whose inner aspects do not match up with their outer aspects, are typically weak people devoid of courage and willpower. They behave treacherously with others, as well as with themselves. There is no one more dangerous than them in the society because they manifest something that is non-existent within themselves. They show a very beautiful outer appearance, while their inner reality is corrupt and polluted.

[29] *Biḥār al-Anwār*, Vol. 15.

Taking Lessons and Guidance

Imām ʿAlī ﷺ has said:

Take lessons from your predecessors before those who proceed you take lessons from you.[30]

History is full of lessons for humankind. It is full of guidance, words of wisdom, and good counsel. It is also full of examples of oppression, controversy, disunity, civilizational decline, and a lack of awareness toward one's environment and time period. In the midst of all this, Imām ʿAlī ﷺ is telling us to take lessons and guidance from those who lived before us, and not allow ourselves to become a lesson for generations to come on how things certain should or should not have been done.

Life is quickly passing by us, so we must take advantage of the time that we have left on this earth.

[30] *Nahj al-Balāghah*, Sermon 31.

LESSON THIRTY

Speech and Silence

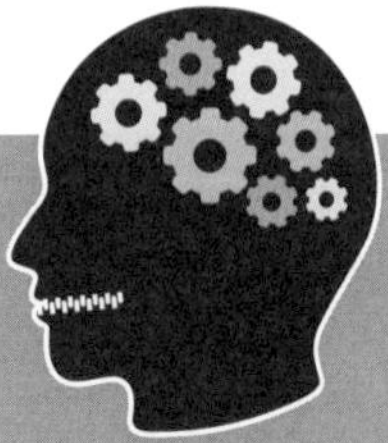

Imām ʿAlī has said:

There is no benefit in the silence of the knowledgeable ones, just as there is no benefit in the speech of the ignorant ones.[31]

Allah has taken a covenant from those who know not to remain silent when they witness people committing sins or deviations taking place. They must use logic and reasoning in order to guide the people to the truth. Everyone is responsible to the degree of their knowledge. Similarly, those who do not know should not interfere in such matters, or else they will simply make a bad situation worse.

It is wrong for knowledgeable people to be silent, just as it is wrong for ignorant individuals to speak in regards to what they do not know.

[31] *Nahj al-Balāghah*, Short Saying 471.

The Pleasure of Forgiveness

Prophet Muḥammad ﷺ has said:

When you become victorious over your enemy, make forgiveness and pardon the tax that is due upon such a victory.[32]

From the Islamic perspective, every blessing that Allah ﷻ has given to us has its own kind of tax. In line with this concept, the tax of power is forgiveness and pardon. Such a tax becomes due when the heart of the enemy is purified from the hatred and animosity that one previously had. When the original root of that opposition is eliminated, then that is when the tax must be paid.

When this forgiveness is freely given, you will see that the same person who hated you yesterday suddenly becomes your closest friend and ally. It is at this time that true victory is achieved—when one is victorious in both the physical realm, and the inner and unseen realms. At the same time, those who quickly seek out revenge are not only deprived of this great virtue, but they also put their victory in danger as well.

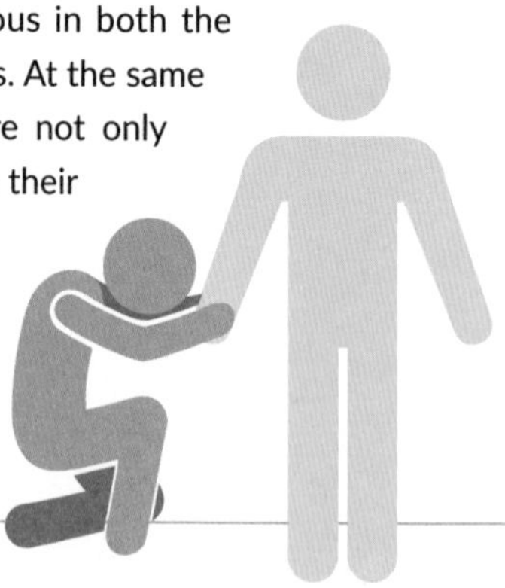

[32] *The Words of Muḥammad* ﷺ.

The True Meaning of Asceticism

Imām ʿAlī has said:

The true ascetic in this world is one whose resistance (against what is unlawful) is not overcome by the allure of unlawful wealth, while the lawful wealth does not take one away from the remembrance of Allah and one's duty of being thankful toward Him.[33]

Some people have distorted the true meaning of the term ascetic (zāhid) and transformed it into a very negative concept. They have redefined this term to refer to someone who distances oneself from all material things and economic activities, and lives like the needy and poverty stricken. Such a concept is incorrect, for true asceticism is that which was lived by the Ahl al-Bayt.

The aforementioned tradition can be divided into two main points. The first is that a person must resist and close one's eyes to all forms of unlawful wealth. The second is that a person should never forget the responsibilities that come with lawful wealth. If people were to define asceticism in this manner, then this would be a progressive form of asceticism that is positive for the society at large. This is opposite to false asceticism, which is undoubtedly a negative and destructive form for society.

[33] *Tuḥaf al-ʿUqūl.*

The Same Rank as Martyrs

Imām ʿAlī has said:

One who fights in the way of Allah and is martyred is not greater than the one who has the ability to sin but keeps oneself pure.[34]

According to Islam, the greatest struggle is that which a person performs against one's own rebellious desires, and this is particularly true in a polluted social environment. Even when people are fighting against a dangerous enemy who seeks to destroy them, this fight will never be successful unless the defenders possess sincerity and unity. If the defenders are entangled in selfishness and disunity, then they will never be able to overcome their enemy.

It is for this same reason that Imām ʿAlī also mentioned that those who fight against their desires and lusts and keep themselves pure in a corrupt environment are no less in rank than those who are martyred fighting in the way of Allah. In *Nahj al-Balāghah*, it has been mentioned that such people are placed in the ranks of the Heavenly angels.

[34] *Nahj al-Balāghah*, Short Saying 474.

LESSON THIRTY-FOUR

The Best of People

Imām ʿAlī ﷺ has said:

The best of people are those who judge with truth.[35]

Proper judgment in issues related to society, the law, and morality is only possible when a person leaves aside one's own personal biases and grudges, and looks out for the true interests of the people. Such a trait is only possible in someone who possesses the light of faith and human virtue.

Furthermore, a person must truly feel for people without being affected by personal interests and biases. These are the ones who are worthy of being considered as 'best of the people.'

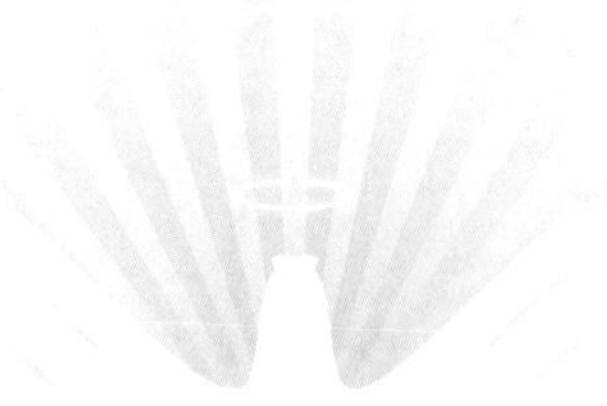

light of faith

human virtue

[35] *Islam dar Qalbe Ijtimāʿ* (Islam in the Heart of the Society).

Photo: imamhussain.org

LESSON THIRTY-FIVE

The Worship of the Free Ones

Imām aṣ-Ṣādiq ﷺ has said:

The worshipers are of three groups. There are those who worship Allah ﷻ out of fear of the Hellfire, and this is the worship of the slaves. Then, there are those who worship Allah ﷻ for the rewards (that are offered), and this is the worship of the wage earners. Then there are those who worship Allah ﷻ out of their love and affection for Him, and this is the worship of the free ones.[36]

Allah's promise is true in that He will reward some people and punish others based on their actions. His reward, and His punishment, will be extraordinary in scope. In spite of this, the 'free ones' see through these rewards, and look at Allah ﷻ alone. They seek nothing but Allah ﷻ, and they fill their hearts only with His love. Their eyes look at something much greater than a simple reward or punishment, and their goal in life is only to truly worship Allah ﷻ and become closer to Him. Thus, their worship of Allah ﷻ is based on their love and understanding of Him.

[36] *Wasāʾil ash-Shīʿah.* This tradition has been similarly narrated by Imām ʿAlī ﷺ.

What Breaks the Back

Imām al-Bāqir ﷺ has said:

There are three things that break a person's back: counting one's good actions as being immense in scale, forgetting one's sins, and being obstinate in one's personal opinions.[37]

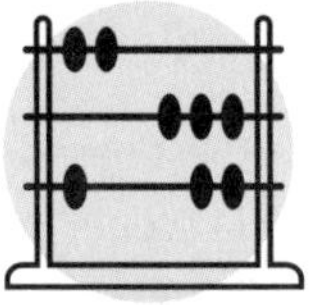

Those people who count their good deeds as being immense in scale will surely become satisfied with them, no matter how few or how small they happen to be. This will act as a barrier against further growth and progress. Those who forget their sins and did not repent for them will continue to commit new ones until they end up destroying themselves. Those who only rely upon their own opinions will be deprived of the collective intellect of their society. They will not benefit from the many forms of knowledge that others possess. As a result, they will soon be overtaken by their mistakes and destroyed with the passing of time.

[37] *Wasā'il ash-Shī'ah*, Vol. 1, P. 73.

Have a Pure Mouth

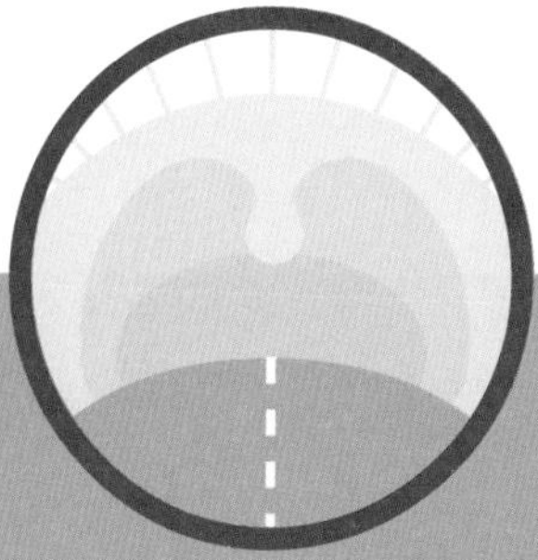

Prophet Muḥammad ﷺ has said:

Your mouths are one of the pathways toward Allah, and the most beloved mouth in front of Allah is the one that is the best smelling. So, make your mouths sweet-smelling as much as possible.[38]

This tradition has both an inner and outer meaning in regards to our mouths. The outer meaning relates to the fact that we use our mouths to get closer to Allah and better ourselves by reciting the verses of the Qur'ān and various supplications. Therefore, we have to be careful about keeping our mouths clean and pleasant smelling.

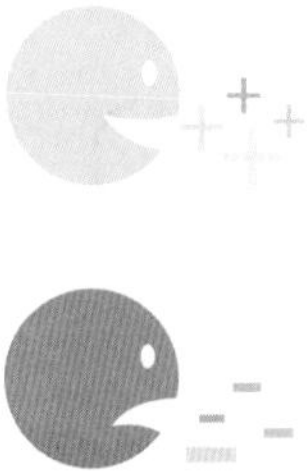

The inner meaning of this tradition is referring to the fact that we use our mouths as a means of communicating with others. Just as we can speak words that will have a positive impact on others, we can also say negative things that can hurt them. These negative forms of speech, such as lying, insulting, slandering, and backbiting pollute our mouths in a spiritual manner. As our mouths become increasingly polluted, we become less able to use them to connect with our Creator (as well as with others).

Keeping our mouths physically and spiritually clean is one of the important pathways toward becoming closer to our Lord.

[38] *Wasāʾil ash-Shīʿah*, Vol. 1, P. 358.

The End Results of Ignorance

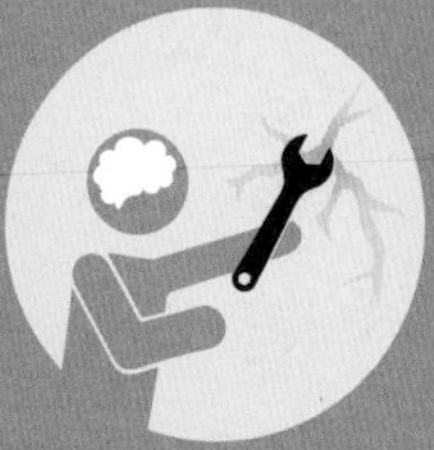

Imām al-Jawād has said:

One who acts without knowledge and awareness will destroy more than what one fixes.[39]

One of the issues related to ignorance and not having the necessary knowledge is that it prevents human beings from reaching the true meaning and full potential of their lives. However, it is not only limited to this, as it can also bring about a great deal of corruption and destruction. For example, in certain situations, an individual may intend to help one's child, but ends up hurting them instead. Someone may want to serve the cause of Islam and humanity, but in reality disgraces the religion and the human race. A person may want to resolve a conflict that has erupted, but only makes things worse. In everything that they do, they make things worse, rather than make them better as a result of their lack of knowledge and awareness.

[39] *Muntahā al-Āmāl.*

LESSON THIRTY-NINE

The Foundations of Guidance

Imām al-Jawād has said:

Faithful believers are in need of three things: divine favor, counsel that arises from the heart, and the acceptance of other people's advice.[40]

Human beings tread a path that is full of ups and downs and filled with many dangers. In order to transform oneself into an effective and beneficial member of society, a person must first develop a spiritual connection with one's Lord. This connection will awaken the individual, and in turn, guide and advise them in their day-to-day affairs. In addition to this inner guiding voice, such a person will also need to listen to the advice and counsel of others in order to draw upon their collective experience and wisdom, which in turn will prove to be invaluable when dealing with new or complex situations.

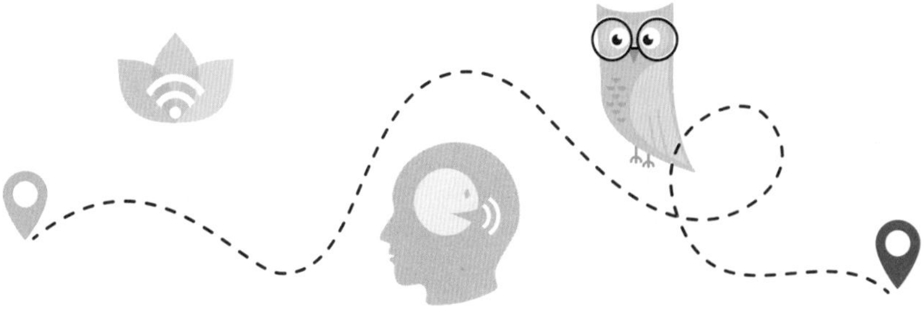

[40] *Muntahā al-Āmāl.*

Lamentation in the Age of Ignorance

Imām al-Bāqir ﷺ is narrated to have reported a saying of Prophet Muḥammad ﷺ, which no one had mentioned before him, which is as follows:

Excessive lamentations are one of the actions from the Age of Ignorance (the time before the advent of Islam).[41]

This tradition is brief, but it contains both an inner and outer meaning. The outer meaning pertains to those actions which people used to perform and were prevalent during the Age of Ignorance. When someone would pass away, the women would cry and lament their death to the extent that they would say false things about the individual. In reality, they would make up lies about the person, which was an inappropriate and deviant form of mourning.

Another possible meaning that Imām al-Bāqir ﷺ may have intended is that when a person faces personal or social problems, one should not just sit down and excessively wail over their difficulties, rather one should ask Allah ﷻ for help, and utilize one's energy and intellect to try and deal with the issues that one faces.

[41] *Wasāʾil ash-Shīʿah*, Vol. 1, P. 915.

LESSON FORTY-ONE

Account for Your Actions Every Day

Imām al-Kāẓim has said:

One who does not account (for one's actions) each day is not from us.[42]

The only possible way to prevent harm to ourselves and work toward further progress is to sit down each day and account for everything we said or did that day. Growth is not possible except through such detailed accounting, and this pertains to both the young and the old. It is actually surprising that people spend so much time accounting for their financial state, or looking after their physical well-being, yet when it comes to their moral and spiritual accounting, they are completely negligent. It is frightening that some individuals spend absolutely no time accounting for their spiritual state during the span of their entire lifetime.

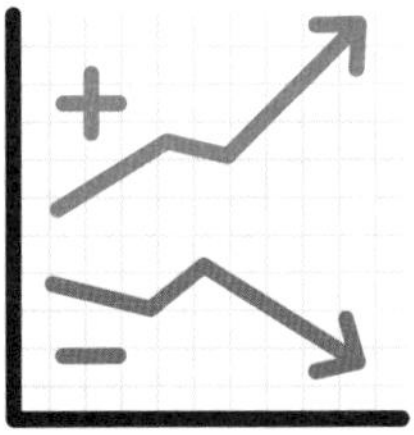

On the other hand, a responsible and aware believer is one who lives by the words of Imām al-Kāẓim in the aforementioned tradition. They account for their actions and deeds every single day. If a person performed something good, they attempt to further it in scope; and if they did something bad, they ask Allah for forgiveness. Over time, such accounting will increase the good that a person does and decrease the evil at an exponential level.

[42] *Aqwāl al-A'immah*, Vol. 1, P. 214.

Faith is More Powerful than Iron

Imām aṣ-Ṣādiq ﷺ has said:

People with faith are stronger than pieces of iron, for when iron is placed into a fire, it changes, but if the believers are killed, brought back to life, and then killed again, no change will be found in their hearts.[43]

Life is composed of various difficulties and complicated issues. People who have low levels of resistance are quickly brought down to their knees in the face of these difficulties. But those who have strong faith are filled with a spirit of resistance and perseverance. Such people will never surrender in the face of difficulties, they will persevere until the very end.

People who possess faith understand that when they are walking on the path of obedience to Allah ﷻ, away from all types of sins, then such a path will naturally have its share of problems and difficulties. Anything worthwhile in life will have trials and obstacles and cannot be easily reached. One must be prepared to put in a lot of hard work, persevere, and self-sacrifice in order to reach high ranks. A person must stand up firmly against one's own rebellious desires, and by doing so, one will be able to achieve a decisive victory.

[43] *Safīnat al-Biḥār*, Vol. 1, P. 37.

The Reality of Monotheism and Divine Justice

Imām ʿAlī has said:

The reality of Allah's Oneness is that you should not limit His Essence to your imagination, and faith in His justice is that you should not accuse Him in regards to anything.[44]

Allah's existence is clear and manifest for us in this world, and even the smallest things are a reminder and proof of His greatness. At the same time, the reality of His Essence (Dhāt) is hidden to us because He is an existence without any limitations, and therefore He is higher than our limited understanding. Thus, we must consider His Essence to be higher than anything we can possibly imagine.

The second issue discussed in this tradition is Allah's justice, where it is explained that everything which takes place in this world happens based on precise rules and for specific reasons. Therefore, we should never look at anything that happens with a negative viewpoint or think that Allah has done something improper or wrong. Such an opinion of Allah is not in concordance with faith and belief in His absolute perfection.

[44] *Nahj al-Balāghah*, Short Saying 470.

Various Signs of Faith

Imām aṣ-Ṣādiq ﷺ has said:

A believing individual's help is valuable, their expenses are little, they live prudently (living according to plan), and they are never bitten the same way twice.[45]

Faith has various signs that can be intellectual, moral, or social in nature. This tradition mentions four signs that should be present in those who have faith.

The first sign states that those who have faith help their fellow human beings, and their assistance is of great value. The reason behind this is because they act based on love, awareness, and complete sincerity toward others. This type of help is exponentially greater than help based on other motivations.

[45] *Safīnat al-Biḥār.*

The second sign is that such people live a simple lifestyle far away from show and ostentation. Lifestyles of showing off naturally bring about a pressure which can cause people to engage in sinful behavior in order to reach their financial goals.

The third sign is that people of faith live their lives planning things out in an organized manner, and this relates to financial matters as well.

The fourth sign is that whenever something goes wrong, they learn from their mistakes and are not harmed or affected by the same thing again.

MENTAL SAMURAI
SEPHORA
tkts

LESSON FORTY-FIVE

This Worldly Life is Not the Goal—It is Simply the Means!

Imām ʿAlī has said:

This world has been created for another purpose, not for its own sake.[46]

Some people become confused when they see certain verses of the Qurʾān and traditions praising the world and mentioning how it is the 'marketplace of the saints,' while other traditions mention the complete opposite, censuring the world and considering it a dangerous and deceptive realm. Such verses and traditions seem to contradict one another.

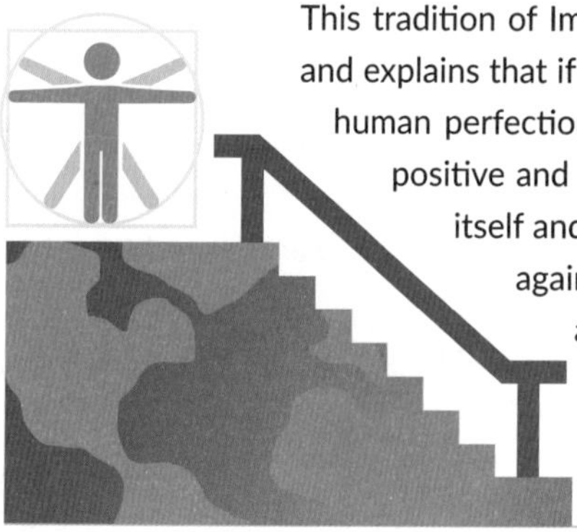

This tradition of Imām ʿAlī clears up this misunderstanding and explains that if this world is taken as a means for reaching human perfection and growth, then it becomes something positive and beloved. However, if it becomes an end in itself and the means of sin, arrogance, and rebellion against Allah, then it will be the most hated and dangerous thing possible.

[46] *Safīnat al-Biḥār*, Vol. 1.

LESSON FORTY-SIX

The Value of Human Beings

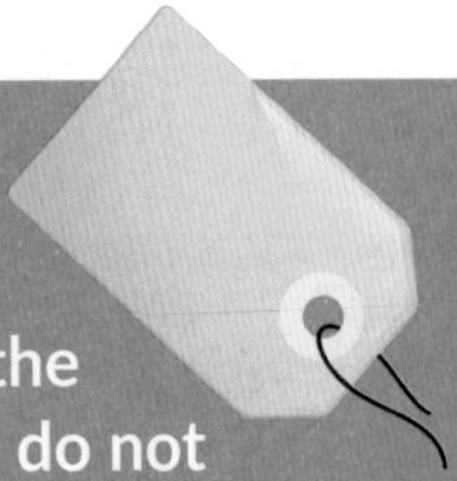

Imām ʿAlī has said:

Know that your souls are worthy of only the everlasting felicity of Paradise; therefore, do not sell yourself short for anything less (than this).[47]

If someone was asked how much they felt their life was worth, they would typically consider it as being priceless. The reality is that our lives are so precious that we cannot even fathom an amount we would be willing to sell it for. Unfortunately, the truth is that most people sell their lives for things of meager value every single day. At the end of their lives, they will see that they gave away their entire lifespan for things like a home, a car, and a few other trinkets. Such people in reality, exchanged the very essence of their lives for things of little to no value. Interestingly enough, they realize that they must soon leave even these inconsequential things, which they spent their entire lives working for.

Here, Imām ʿAlī is telling us that there is nothing in this world which is more worthy than our souls. The only thing worth this grand amount is the pleasure of Allah, and the perfection and completion of ourselves as human beings. Even if we were to exchange the entirety of our lives for the pleasure of Allah and the reward of Paradise, it would be well worth it. In fact, such an exchange is the only thing which can be considered a proper trade for our life's work.

[47] *Nahj al-Balāghah*, Short Saying 456.

LESSON FORTY-SEVEN

Truth and Falsehood

Imām ʿAlī has said:

The truth is heavy and difficult, yet it is refreshing and agreeable; while falsehood is light and easy, but painful and dangerous.[48]

This description of truth and falsehood by Imām ʿAlī is extremely brief in terms of words, yet exceedingly eloquent. The tradition mentions that although truth may initially seem difficult to deal with, it is in reality, one of the best things for people to hear. Truth is like a healing balm which can cure society of its many ills and problems.

On the other hand, falsehood is easier to deal with initially, thus many people may prefer to hear what is false rather than the truth. Yet, by its very nature, falsehood acts like a poison that damages and destroys whatever it comes into contact with. It can be compared to some kind of food that looks delicious, but is actually filled with poison. It may taste good with those first bites, but very soon, the destructive effects of the poison can be felt, and the person will suffer greatly as a result of it.

[48] *Biḥār al-Anwār*, Vol. 70, P. 107.

LESSON FORTY-EIGHT

The Most Valuable Legacy of the Arabs

Prophet Muḥammad ﷺ has said:

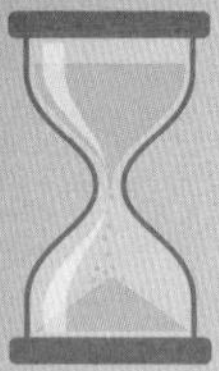

The most correct and far-reaching sentence that the Arabs have mentioned can be found in the words of Lubayd (a famous Arab poet) when he said: 'Know that everything except Allah ﷻ is void and useless, and every blessing will eventually slip through your hands.'[49]

The finite nature of wealth and social position, as well as their inevitable loss, teaches us that we should be careful to earn them in lawful and just ways, and we should also be cautious to spend them moderately and lawfully.

We should understand that the *only* infinite existence is that of Allah ﷻ, and we all exist due to His mercy.

This thought should be enough to keep us humble and focused while we are living in this world.

[49] *Miṣbāh al-Sharī'ah*, P. 45.

I am Weary and Disgusted of Them

Imām ar-Riḍā ؑ has said:

One who cheats, harms, or tricks another Muslim is not from us.[50]

Those who find happiness in the dispossession of others and think they will benefit by such things cannot be considered true Muslims; in fact, they cannot even be regarded as proper human beings. What makes human beings superior to other creations is found in their social behavior; those people who seek benefit in the harm of others are lacking in this important human element. In some cases, people may try to harm others openly, while others may attempt to do so quietly and in a hidden way. Islam has forbidden all such types of behavior that harms others. Imām ar-Riḍā ؑ has said: "I am a stranger to those who commit such actions."

[50] *Safīnat al-Biḥār*, Ghash (adulteration).

Efforts of the Weak

Imām ʿAlī ﷺ has said:

Backbiting is the last resort of the weak.[51]

Amongst the greater sins, there are a few sins which display the sinner's weakness and wretched nature, and backbiting is one of these sins. Those who gather together in order to seek out the faults of others and make their shortcomings public are guilty of this grave sin. The fact of the matter is that most people are not without fault, and virtually everyone has some weakness or another.

The question remains that why do people resort to backbiting then? The answer is that these individuals act in this way in order to soothe the feelings of jealousy and enmity which they have against others. People who engage in such behavior are those who are so weak that they cannot confront others in a direct fashion, so they engage in this cowardly and indirect attack. They are only capable of stabbing people in the back by backbiting them. It has been mentioned in the traditions that if a person who backbites others repents for one's sins, then they will be the last of the people to enter Paradise; and if that person does not repent, then they will be the first of those to enter the Hellfire.

[51] *Nahj al-Balāghah*, Short Saying 461.

LESSON FIFTY-ONE

Signs of the Oppressors

Imām ʿAlī ﷺ has said:

Oppressors have three signs: (1) they oppress those who are above them through opposition and disobedience, (2) they oppress those who are below them through domination and compulsion, and (3) they cooperate with other oppressors.[52]

Those people who possess a spirit of oppression will always exhibit facets of this spirit through their actions. When they are supposed to obey the commands of those above them, they rebel and disobey them. When they find people who are employed by them or under their command, then they act in a forceful way and put them under pressure. The third sign is that they cooperate and collaborate with those who are oppressors as well. Their friends and close associates all possess the characteristics of oppressors as well. In a nutshell, such individuals are oppressors in all aspects of their lives and character, and it can clearly be seen that the attribute of oppression has taken over their entire being.

[52] *Nahj al-Balāghah*, Short Saying 350.

There is No Disease Without a Cure

Prophet Muḥammad ﷺ has said:

Allah ﷻ has not created any pain (or disease) except that He also created its cure.[53]

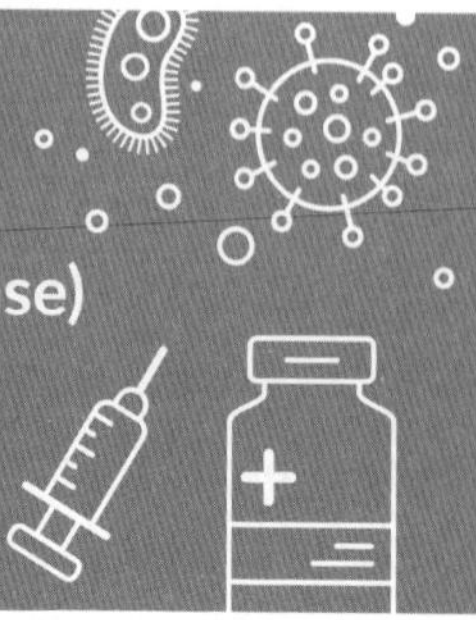

The world that we live in is composed of various actions and reactions, and everything that lies on one extreme possesses a relationship with something that lies on the other extreme. For example, when we have the phenomenon of cold in this world, there also exists warmth and heat. When there is anger, there is also calm. In this same way, there is a cure to be found for every disease that exists; the only issue is that it must be sought out and found, just like a warm blanket needs to be sought out in the face of the cold.

[53] *Nahj al-Faṣāḥah.*

There is no disease that cannot be cured in this world—be it physical, mental, emotional, social, or spiritual.

This does not only apply to problems of the physical body; it also applies to social and spiritual problems. Some people believe that various things are unsolvable, so when they see an issue, they just leave it alone, thinking that it must be tolerated with no possible solution. These people are negligent of the reality that every pain and every disease possesses its own cure; and in fact, there is no disease that cannot be cured in this world—be it physical, mental, emotional, social, or spiritual. Therefore, we must persevere and work hard when faced with the pains and problems of life, and seek a way toward their resolution and cure.

LESSON FIFTY-THREE

That Which Destroys Blessings

Imām al-Bāqir has said:

Allah made a decisive rule that He will never take away a blessing that He has given to people unless they commit a sin which causes the loss of that blessing.[54]

The blessings of Allah are endless, but it cannot be said that they are given without calculation. Allah never bestows anything to anyone without proper accounting, and He never takes something away without a valid reason.

When people begin to use the blessings of Allah as a means of corruption, arrogance, and oppression, then those same blessings will be transformed into a means of their destruction. It is at this time when the blessing is removed that a calamity will come in its place.

When such a thing happens, positive phenomena like industry and technology will be turned into destructive elements. Society will begin to fall apart, and these blessings will become the cause of worry and anxiety. Even things that are supposed to help people and allow them to be more efficient will become the means of their regression. This is all due to the improper use of Allah's blessings.

[54] *Uṣūl al-Kāfī*, Vol. 2.

Martyrdom and Purity

Prophet Muḥammad ﷺ has said:

If you leave this world in a state of (spiritual) purity, then you will be counted as being among the martyrs.[55]

This tradition is part of the commands that the Prophet ﷺ gave to his companion Anas. He said to him: "If you are able to be in a state of (spiritual) purity (wuḍū') day and night, then be as such. This is because if you were to leave this world in such a state, then you will be (considered) a martyr." This tradition is primarily referring to the state of ritual purity known as wuḍū', but it also refers to a more important reality which is living a pure life and dying a pure death.

Those whose thoughts, bodies, and lives are pure, and they end up dying in this state are, without a doubt, in the same ranks as the martyrs.

Other traditions from the Ahl al-Bayt also emphasize this same reality.

[55] *Safīnat al-Biḥār*, Vol. 1, P. 720.

Photo: Hassan Roholamin (shiaarts.ir)

LESSON FIFTY-FIVE

The Self-Sacrificing Lovers

Imām al-Bāqir has said:

The self-sacrificing companions of my grandfather, Imām Ḥusayn, did not feel any pain under the striking swords or the piercing spears of the enemies.[56]

When an individual loves something intensely, all of their senses will be focused on the object of their love. It is for this reason that any difficulty they face will be considered as nothing at all; in fact, they will not even feel any of these tribulations while in that state. When the women of Egypt saw Prophet Yūsuf and his beauty, they all cut their hands under the effect of this attraction and love. They were so taken in that they could not even feel themselves cutting deep into their hands, whereas this is something that should have caused them immense pain under normal conditions.

Those who are taken in by the love of Allah will not feel the immense pain of any sacrifice that they undertake in His way.

[56] *Biḥār al-Anwār*, Vol. 45, P. 80.

LESSON FIFTY-SIX

The Wise and the Foolish

Imām 'Alī ﷺ has said:

The wise depend on their hard work and actions, while the foolish depend on their hopes and desires.[57]

People with wisdom live their lives based on a code of positivity and seeking the truth, and it is for this reason that they go after their goals with solid planning, rather than simply relying on their imagination and dreams. It is not possible to achieve one's goals without hard work and struggle; therefore, one must truly persevere and be constant in their efforts.

Foolish people, on the other hand, sit around floating in their hopes and dreams. They do not put forth any effort and only imagine the things they want to do or who they want to be. They gain pleasure out of these thoughts, and since there is no effort required for conjuring up such ideas, they never end up doing anything. In spite of this, they are always in expectation of victory over their imaginary goals, but of course without hard work and effort, they will never be able to achieve any of their dreams.

[57] *Ghurar al-Ḥikam.*

plan
wise
truth
work hard
positive
struggle
persevere
constant
imaginary goals
foolish
dream
floating
expectation
no effort
thoughts
hope

The Truly Religious are Few in Number

Imām Ḥusayn ﷺ has said:

Many people are slaves of this world, and religion is something present only on their tongues. As long as their lives are going well under the protection of their religion, they support it, but when difficulties come and they are tested, the truly religious are few in number.[58]

Religion, particularly the religion of Islam, protects the rights of people in society. It supports what is truly in their best interests and enacts justice in the society. In some situations, religion can go against the personal interests of various people. It is here that the truly religious and those who are simply posing as being religious can be differentiated.

What we mean by this is that some people are only after their own personal interests, and they are only religious as long as it benefits them materially. As soon as upholding the religion becomes a cause for material loss, they completely leave it. The truly religious are those who are loyal to their faith regardless of whether it is to their material benefit or loss at that point in time. Faith is their major driving force, not personal or material interests.

[58] *Biḥār al-Anwār*, Vol. 10, P. 198.

Justice and Fairness Between One's Children

Prophet Muḥammad ﷺ has said:

Be fair when it comes to your children just as you would like them to be fair when it comes to you.[59]

A major problem that some people have is not being just when it comes to their children. In some families, the eldest child is treated differently and considered as being superior to the rest. In other cases, the youngest child is spoiled and given more attention than the rest. In these situations, the parents give all of their love, affection, and care to one of their children, and create differences in how the rest of them are treated. This may cause anger and animosity among the siblings, which could lead them to become jealous and resentful of one another. In addition, they may hold grudges against the parents, which end up manifesting later on in life when the parents have become old and are in need of their children's help.

[59] *Biḥār al-Anwār*, Vol. 23.

LESSON FIFTY-NINE

You are Always Being Watched!

Imām al-Jawād ﷺ has said:

Know that you are never outside the sight of Allah ﷻ, so be careful how you behave.[60]

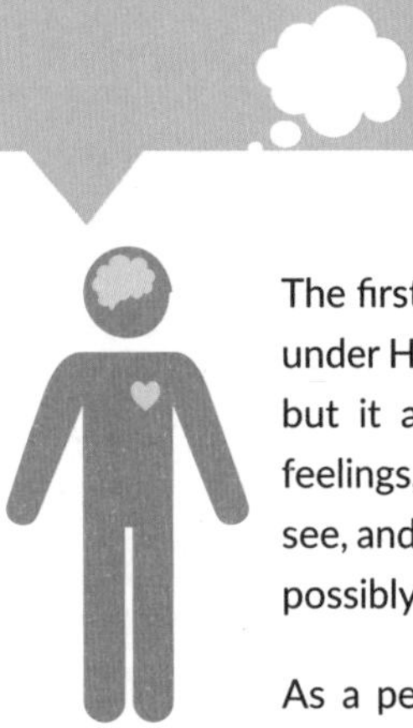

The first effect of faith in Allah ﷻ is knowing that you are constantly under His watch. This is not just a sense of physically being watched, but it also relates to one's inner state, such as one's thoughts, feelings, and intentions. There is nothing that the Almighty does not see, and this is the most comprehensive sense of being seen that can possibly exist.

As a person's faith grows stronger, the sense of this observation also increases, becoming more comprehensive and deeper in scope. This continues until an individual sees oneself as being perpetually under watch. This state is the greatest and most powerful means of self and social reformation, and it is the most beautiful manifestation of faith. Knowing this reality can also help cure the worst social ills which are present in our society today.

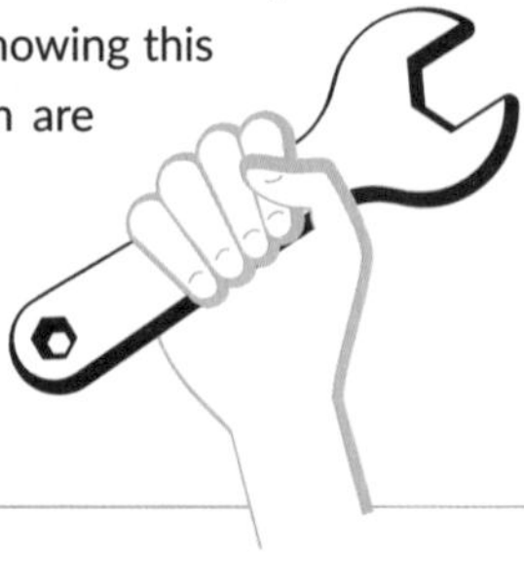

[60] *Tuḥaf al-'Uqūl.*

LESSON SIXTY

Neither Envy, Nor Flattery

Imām ʿAlī ﷺ has said:

Praising people beyond what they are worthy of is flattery, and praising them less than what they deserve is either an inability to express oneself or it is envy.[61]

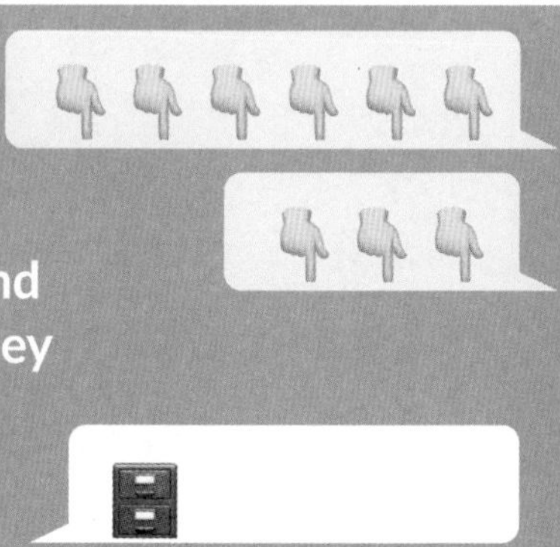

There is no doubt that we should praise those people who perform worthy actions or possess noble attributes. Such individuals should be supported and encouraged in the path that they have chosen. At the same time, this must be done in a balanced manner. If it is done excessively, then it will be considered flattery, which will also bring down the praiser's character; and cause the rise of egoism and conceit in the person who is being praised. If such an action is performed less than what the person is worthy of, then it will also have negative consequences because the individual will become discouraged. This is a sign of either envy or an inability to express oneself on the part of the one who was giving the praise.

[61] *Nahj al-Balāghah*, Short Saying 347.

Be in the Service of Your Fellow Believers

Imām aṣ-Ṣādiq has said:

A person who helps fulfill the needs of one's religious brothers (or sisters) will find that Allah will help them in fulfilling their own needs.[62]

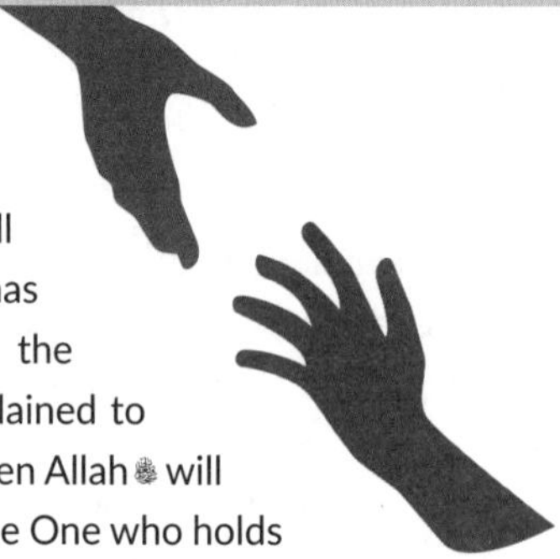

People typically think that if they were to help others resolve their problems, then they would fall behind and not progress in their own lives. Islam has explained that the reality is other than this, and the Imām, in the aforementioned tradition, has explained to us that if we help our fellow believers in religion, then Allah will help us with the problems that we face. Allah is the One who holds true power and is able to help us with all of our issues. This is something which many people have experienced in their own lives as well. Whenever they help others overcome their problems, they are helped in resolving their own difficulties. In some cases, this help comes in strange and unexpected ways, and there is no doubt that this is a form of Divine mercy and help.

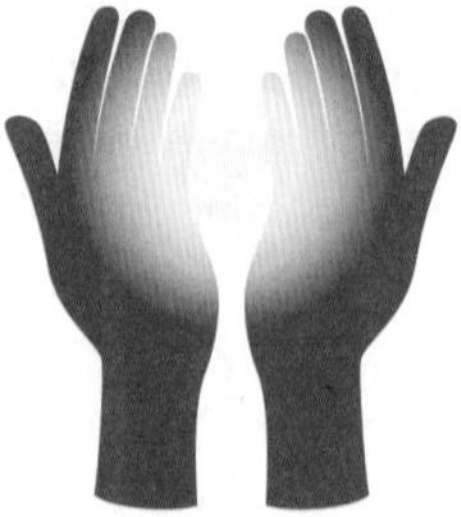

[62] *Biḥār al-Anwār*, Vol. 74, P. 286.

LESSON SIXTY-TWO

Mistakes in Life

Imām ʿAlī has said:

Do not busy your heart with sorrow over what has already passed, or else you will not be sufficiently prepared for what is to come (in the future).[63]

There is virtually no one (except for the 14 Maʿṣūmīn) who has never committed any mistakes in their lives, nor missed some good opportunities. In reality, people can be divided into two main groups: There are those who are always sorrowful over what has taken place in the past, and expend a great deal of energy reminiscing over what could have been. The second group is composed of individuals who consider what has passed to be in the past and basically let go of what took place beforehand, only taking lessons from these events for their future. This group then mobilizes all of their energy and power toward building their present and the future. There is no doubt that the best method of living is in what Imām ʿAlī has mentioned in this tradition.

[63] *Ghurar al-Ḥikam*, P. 289.

LESSON SIXTY-THREE

Islam will be the Religion of the World

Prophet Muḥammad ﷺ has said:

There will not remain any home on this Earth, even homes made of earth or woolen tents, except that Allah ﷻ will allow Islam to enter into those homes.[64]

Every day it is becoming more and more manifest that the religion of Islam is the best religion on the face of this earth. People are realizing that either they must leave religion completely aside, or they must accept Islam as the true and final religion sent down by Allah ﷻ. Since religion is an integral part of human nature and our intrinsic selves, it follows that people cannot simply leave aside religion altogether. The only real option that they have left among the various religions is that of Islam. This phenomenon can be seen in our modern day world by the ever-increasing number of people who are accepting Islam as their religion. Islam has spread to virtually every nation on this Earth, and masājid (mosques) can be found even in far-flung regions and cities throughout the world.

With that said, it must be mentioned that the completion of this transformation will only take place with the appearance of the twelfth savior, Imām al-Mahdī عج. When he comes, polytheism and idol worshiping will be completely destroyed and Islam will manifest itself throughout the entire world. This is the reality which the Prophet ﷺ gave glad tidings about in the above tradition.

[64] *Majmaʿ al-Bayān*, Commentary on Sūrah at-Tawbah.

Do Not Consider Any Sin as Being Small in Nature

Imām Ḥasan al-ʿAskarī has said:

Among the sins which are unforgivable is when a person says: 'I wish I would only be punished for this one sin.'[65]

In Islam, it is possible for lesser sins to be transformed into greater sins.

One such way is when an individual considers the lesser sins as being small and inconsequential in nature. This in fact is, one of the dangerous insinuations that Shayṭān makes to people where he tells them that their sins are actually nothing to worry about because they are of no real value or significance. In certain cases, greater sins which create fear and worry in people, can actually pose a lesser risk because people quickly recognize them and work to avoid them wholeheartedly. With lesser sins, there is always the risk that a person may discount them and see them as being trivial in nature. When such sins are committed repeatedly, they are then transformed into greater sins. Such sins will be the cause of great torment and difficulty for people—both in this world and the next. They become greater sins because in a way, one is breaking the sanctity of Allah by repeatedly and purposefully disobeying Him and doing what He has forbidden.

[65] *Tuḥaf al-ʿUqūl*, P. 366.

The Superiority of Knowledge

Imām al-Kāẓim has said:

The superiority of a scholar over a worshiper is like the superiority of the sun in relation to the stars.[66]

The stars which are found in the skies possess light in and of themselves, but they are not able to illuminate much else besides themselves. For example, their light is not able to illuminate our homes or walkways on this earth. The sun on the other hand is so powerful that its rays illuminate the earth and everything that exists upon it. It not only possesses intrinsic light, but it also lights the way for billions of human beings, as well as other creatures. This is a light that completely illuminates the roads for us and shows us where we need to go in our lives.

This metaphor can aptly be applied to the differences between a scholar who possesses knowledge, and a worshiper who is devout, but lacks such knowledge. A worshiper only attempts to save oneself, but a scholar is one who strives to save countless individuals. This is truly a monumental difference between these two categories of believers. We should also keep in mind that if it were not for the scholars, then the worshipers would not exist either. It is through the light of the scholars that people are able to find their way and become devout worshipers of Allah.

[66] *Tuḥaf al-'Uqūl*, P. 307.

Mutual Rights

Prophet Muḥammad ﷺ has said:

Just as children are responsible if they do not uphold the rights of their mothers and fathers, similarly, mothers and fathers are also responsible if they do not uphold the rights of their children.[67]

In this world, wherever we find a right that has been enjoined, we will also find a responsibility which has been attached to it. Rights and responsibilities have been created alongside one another, and as the rights increase in scope, the responsibilities become heavier in relation as well. Just as parents have a great right upon their children (a right mentioned in the Qur'ān as being of the same rank as the right that Allah ﷻ has upon us), similarly, children also have certain rights upon their parents.

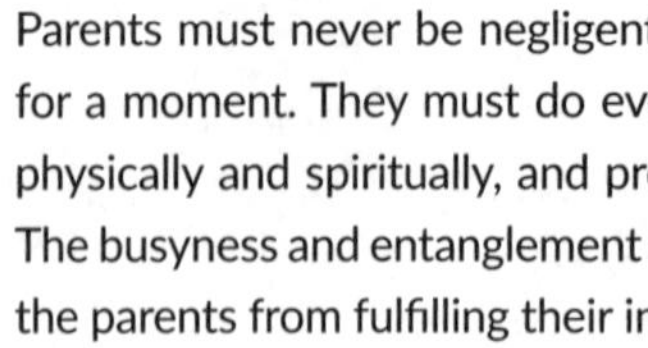

Parents must never be negligent in teaching and educating their children, not even for a moment. They must do everything possible in order to build up their children physically and spiritually, and protect them from intellectual and ethical corruption. The busyness and entanglement of day to day life is no excuse and should not prevent the parents from fulfilling their important responsibilities toward their children.

[67] *Aqwāl al-Aʾimmah.*

LESSON SIXTY-SEVEN

Spend in the Way of Allah's Obedience so that You Do Not Spend in the Way of Sin!

Imām al-Kāẓim ﷺ has said:

Do not abstain from spending money in the way of Allah's obedience, for if you do, then you will inevitably spend twice as much in the way of sin and error.[68]

There are some people who are so stingy when it comes to money that even when they become ill, they refuse to spend anything on treating themselves. As a result, their condition worsens and they are then forced to spend two or three times that amount in curing themselves. This is in fact a general rule that if someone does not spend the necessary money on their basic expenses, then they will in turn be forced to spend much more when an issue comes up later on.

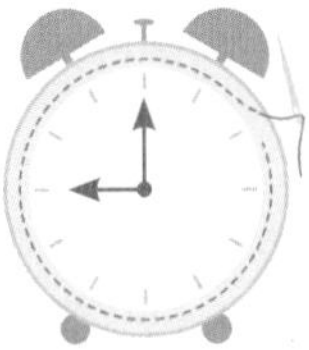

Those who refrain from spending time or money for the education and training of their children could end up paying a backbreaking price later on in life. Such neglect can bring out issues in their children like deviancy, criminality, or drug addiction. The parents will end up suffering a hundred fold for their neglect, which could have been remedied with just a small amount of time and effort. Similarly, if a person neglects to help the poverty stricken of their society, then they may end up paying several times that to prevent various things which could arise later from such miserliness.

[68] *Tuḥaf al-'Uqūl*, P. 305.

The Largest Marketplace

Imām al-Hādī ☙ has said:

The world is a marketplace wherein one group profits, while another group loses.[69]

This world is not the real home of human beings—it is neither a final abode, nor is it a permanent place to stay. In reality, it is a grand marketplace where people invest their resources and hope to gain a return on what they worked so hard for. These resources include their intellectual, emotional, spiritual, and psychological wealth. Accumulating these will lead us toward everlasting felicity and happiness in the next world.

People who are active, hard working, and aware are cognizant of the existence of this grand marketplace, and they are always busy working so that they can 'purchase' valuable goods with the resources they have at hand. Their goal is to transform what they possess into more valuable goods which are everlasting, and they do this for the felicity of both themselves, as well as their society. This is in contradiction to those who sell their resources for goods of lesser value (or in some cases, things which are of a purely corrupted and destructive nature). The end result is that those who 'traded' well will leave this world with a load of true wealth which will last forever, while those who 'traded' improperly will leave this world with nothing in their account but loss and regret.

[69] *Tuḥaf al-ʿUqūl*, P. 361.

The Highest Ranking People

Prophet Muḥammad ﷺ has said:

The most eminent people on the Day of Judgment will be those who took the greatest steps in advising (and seeking the best for) the creations of Allah.[70]

Serving and helping people is considered to be one of the greatest acts of worship in Islam. In fact, one of the ways in which we can serve Allah is to think about the benefits and interests of other people as one's own benefit and interest. Just as one will consider their personal interests with the utmost care and consideration, likewise one should consider the interests of other people in the same way. A person should seek the best for other individuals both in their presence, as well as in their absence.

[70] *Uṣūl al-Kāfī*, Vol. 2, P. 166.

Three Important Social Principles

Imām aṣ-Ṣādiq has said:

All people (in relation to their social rights) are equal to one another much like the teeth of a comb. An individual will become many in number due to their fellow believers (in religion). It is not worthy for a person to sit with someone who does not want for you what they want for themselves.[71]

Three important principles have been mentioned in this tradition. The first is that all human beings are equal to one another in their rights, no matter what their race, language, or social class is. The second principle is that individuals are connected to one another in a society and the society relates back to the individual as well. In this way, all of the believers are what really compose a society overall. The third principle manifests the necessity of wanting for others what one wants for themselves. This is considered a primary principle for the friendship that exists among people. A nation in which these three principles are not upheld will neither be an Islamic nation, nor a nation of true human beings.

[71] *Tuḥaf al-'Uqūl*, P. 274.

1 All human beings are equal to one another
in their rights, no matter their race, language, or social class

2 Individuals are connected to one another
in a society and the society relates back to the individual as well

3 It is necessary for people to want for others what they want for themselves

To be Hot Tempered and Rash

Imām ʿAlī has said:

Being hot tempered and rash is a type of insanity, for the possessor of these attributes quickly becomes regretful over what they have done; and if they do not become regretful, then their insanity has (indeed) become permanent.[72]

Human intellect and understanding necessitates that people should abstain from hastiness and rash behavior. When people act in such a manner, they are left unable to properly analyze or judge a given situation. They soon regret their hasty decision-making and realize that they clearly made a mistake. This is an error which most likely would not have been made if they had properly gauged the situation at hand and not been quick to react.

[72] *Nahj al-Balāghah*, Short Saying 255.

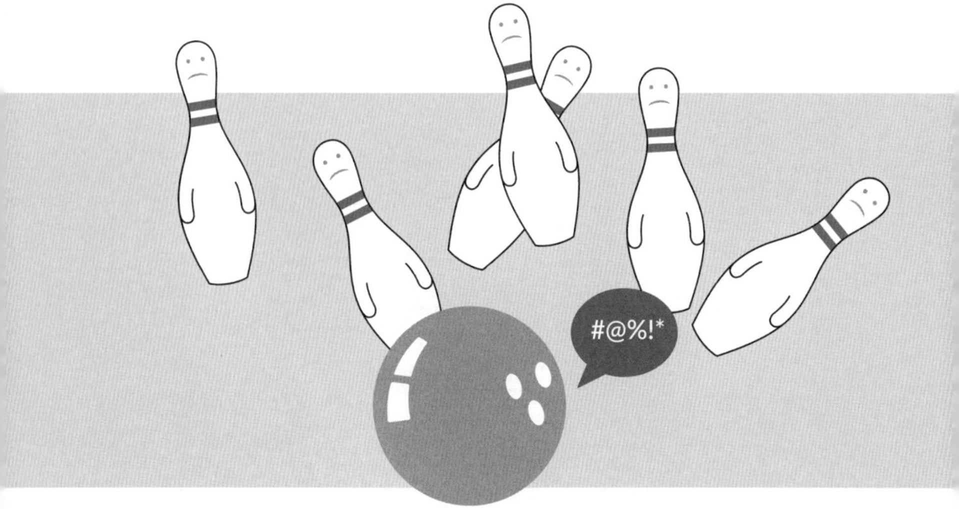

In some cases, people may be rash in their speech and with just a few words, they can destroy a lifetime of careful planning and work. By saying insensitive things, people can lose friends whose friendship they had cultivated over many years of their lives. Such people will be left with only regret and sorrow for their hasty and rash speech. However, if such individuals do not become regretful even after tasting the fruits of their haste, then it is clear that they have been afflicted by a state of insanity.

The True Ascetics

Prophet Muḥammad ﷺ has said:

Asceticism in this world can be found in three things: cutting short one's desires, thankfulness for one's blessings, and abstaining from the unlawful.[73]

Many people do not have a proper understanding of asceticism in Islam; and they understand it to be a life isolated from society and all things related to money and wealth. Due to this idea, they see such a life as one full of hardship and something related to obscure mysticism; they see it as being contrary to progress and societal growth. However, true asceticism is actually a progressive program of life, and it can be instrumental in the building of the overall society. This narration explains how:

True asceticism is actually found in the cutting short of desires, being thankful for one's blessings, and abstinence from what is unlawful.

[73] *Tuḥaf al-'Uqūl*, P. 58.

Examining One's Character

Imām ʿAlī has said:

There are three things through which the intellect of great people is tested: wealth, position, and calamities.[74]

The tests of Allah are a means of allowing human beings to grow and reach perfection in their day to day lives. These tests are never set in stone and are administered in a multitude of different ways. There are three things which are the most important when it comes to people and these are issues related to wealth, social position, and calamities. How will an individual react when given a sum of wealth—will they lose control and begin to act in all sorts of extravagant and excessive ways?

How will a given person act when given a high-ranking social position—will they forget who they really are and become arrogant and proud? How will someone respond when faced with a calamity or difficulty in life? Will they sit in a corner and become utterly despondent, losing their sense of thankfulness toward Allah? These are three of the most important things which human beings will be tested with in their lives.

[74] *Ghurar al-Ḥikam*, Root Section: Thulāth.

LESSON SEVENTY-FOUR

The Way of Working in this Life for the Next

Imām ar-Riḍā ﷺ has said:

Work toward the life of this world as if you will live forever in it, and work toward the next life as if you will die tomorrow.[75]

This tradition details how Islam views our material and spiritual lives both in this world and the next. A Muslim should live one's life in this world in such a firm and established way that it seems as if one is going to live in this world forever. This statement completely destroys the ideology of false asceticism which some people have tried to attribute to Islam.

Similarly, when it comes to spiritual issues and our level of preparedness for the next world, it is necessary to be so exact and detailed that if we were to die tomorrow, we would not have any defiencies or regrets. This means that we constantly cleanse ourselves from any sins with true repentance, and we would have paid back in full anything we owed to other people in terms of their rights. If we live in such a way, then whenever our moment of death comes, we will not be left with any regrets and sorrows over what we should have done.

[75] *Wasā'il ash-Shī'ah* (according to the section Aqwāl al-A'immah) Vol. 2, P. 277.

The Effects of Sins

Imām aṣ-Ṣādiq ﷺ has said:

Those who die as a result of their sins are more than those who die due to their natural life spans; and those who live as a result of their good actions are more than those who live due to their natural life spans.[76]

It has now been proven that a considerable number of physical diseases have their primary roots in various spiritual problems. Similarly, one of the most important factors of psychological disease can be found in issues related to the conscience, and these issues are caused by the performance of sins and the negative effects of these sins on the soul. A sinful person is in reality 'convicted' by one's soul and is likewise punished for what one does. The effects of this punishment can be witnessed on the soul, as well as the physical body. The effects of these sins can even be seen in how and when a person dies, as it can expediate one's death.

Similarly, good actions have their own specific effects on the conscience and the soul. These positive actions bring about spiritual wealth and energy, and they in turn have an effect on the physical body as well, and can influence how long a person lives. In summary, it can be said that sins shorten one's lifespan, while good actions lengthen it.

[76] *Safīnat al-Biḥār.*

The True Shīʿahs

Imām al-Bāqir said to one of his companions:

Tell our Shīʿahs (followers) that no one will attain that which is with Allah except through their actions.[77]

These words of Imām al-Bāqir are an answer to those who imagine that it is enough to simply mention that one is a Shīʿah, or express affection toward the family of the Prophet in order to achieve salvation. Such people believe that one can achieve the greatest rank before Allah simply through this kind of lip service, while we know our status is based on our actions, and the true Shīʿahs are those whose actions are based on the teachings of the Prophet and his Ahl al-Bayt. Therefore, one should realize that the real Shīʿah of the Prophet and his Ahl al-Bayt are those who are truly following in their footsteps, and that words and expressions of love alone are not enough.

[77] *Uṣūl al-Kāfī*, Vol. 2, P. 300.

With Whom Should We Consult?

Imām ʿAlī ﷺ has said:

Do not consult with miserly people for they will restrain you from serving Allah's creation and will make you fear poverty. Do not consult with cowardly people for they will weaken your will toward doing important things; and (similarly) do not consult with greedy people for they will present oppression as something (positive and) beautiful.[78]

To consult with others and seek advice is an important concept that is greatly encouraged in Islam. At the same time, consultation requires certain prerequisites for it to be beneficial. For example, consulting with people who have clear defects in certain aspects will result in receiving ineffective advice. Such advice will actually end up harming you and perhaps others instead of helping the situation. It is for this reason that Imām ʿAlī ﷺ emphasized that a person should not select any of these three categories of people for advice and consultation. The emphasis on this increases as the issue being consulted upon grows in importance.

[78] *Nahj al-Balāghah*, Letter 53.

This tradition mentions that the miserly, the cowardly, and the greedy are among those who should not be consulted with, and the reasoning is that they all impart their own particular worldview to the advice that they give. However, since their worldview is twisted and incorrect, their advice will similarly be distorted and inaccurate as well.

Such people will transform generosity into miserliness, courage into cowardice, and a sense of satisfaction into greed; and they may even encourage the oppression of others in order to reach their own goals.

The Best of Blessings

Imām ʿAlī has said:

The best blessing is health and soundness, while the best thing which can fill one's heart is faith in Allah.[79]

In this tradition, Imām ʿAlī has pointed out the greatest physical and spiritual blessings which one can have. Physical health is not only the greatest material blessing, but it is the root of all other blessings as well. It is through means of our physical health that we are able to do everything else. Without physical health, such things like prayer, fasting, charity, and other good works would not be possible for us to perform.

When it comes to spiritual issues, the greatest blessing that a person can have is a heart filled with faith in Allah. This is something which allows us to see the world as it is, and lights the way in front of us even in the depths of darkness.

It is through faith that the disease of ignorance and sin will be eliminated, and one's heart and body will become calm and peaceful.

[79] *Tuḥaf al-ʿUqūl*, P. 206.

The Hidden Imām عجل الله تعالى فرجه الشريف

Someone asked Imām aṣ-Ṣādiq عليه السلام: "How do the people benefit from the existence of a hidden Imām?" The Imām عليه السلام answered:

In the same way that one benefits from the sun (even) when it is hidden behind the clouds.[80]

The light of the sun is the driving source for all life that exists on this Earth, and there is no living creature which is able to continue its existence in the long term without this amazing source of energy. In this same way, Imām al-Mahdī عجل الله تعالى فرجه الشريف has been likened to the power of the sun over all that exists on this Earth. This does not only apply to their physical existence, but also their spiritual existence as well.

Even when the sun is hidden behind the clouds, it still transmits a great deal of light to the Earth, and this light exerts a significant influence over all living things. Similarly, the Imām عجل الله تعالى فرجه الشريف exerts immense physical and spiritual benefits over the Earth, even when he is hidden from the sight of the people. It must be understood though that all things will benefit only to the degree of their potential.

The benefit of the people from the Imām عجل الله تعالى فرجه الشريف will only be to the degree that they develop themselves and are able to benefit from him.

[80] *Biḥār al-Anwār*, Vol. 52, P. 92.

LESSON EIGHTY

Do Not Join in Every Conversation

Imām al-Jawād ﷺ has said:

One who listens to a speaker has worshiped them. Therefore, if the speaker talks about Allah ﷻ, they have worshiped Allah ﷻ and if they speak about Satan, then they have worshiped Satan.[81]

Whenever a person speaks in regards to a certain topic, they exert a level of influence over those who hear them. Similarly, when an individual listens to another person's speech, one will become influenced by those words as well. Words can be positive or negative, and in some cases, they can be a mixture of both truth and falsehood. When a person sits complacently and listens to someone else's speech, it is a type of worship in the sense that the words take root in one's soul and exert their own influence and effect in different ways.

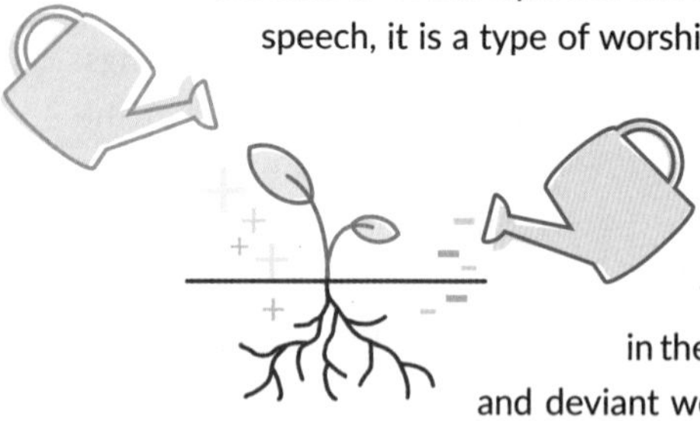

Those who listen to good truthful words will find positivity and honesty taking root in their souls, while those who listen to negative and deviant words will find those attributes taking root in their souls. Therefore, we must always be careful not to engage in the company of negative speakers so that their words do not affect us in a detrimental way.

[81] *Tuḥaf al-'Uqūl*, P. 339.

People with Attributes of Satan

Prophet Muḥammad ﷺ has said:

If you see someone who does not care about what they say or what people say about them, then you should know that they are either corrupt or Satanic (in nature).[82]

When people submerse themselves very deeply in sin, they will eventually reach a point where they no longer care what others say about them or what they say about others. They will mention the worst types of slander in regards to other people, and will be utterly indifferent when similar things are directed toward them. When someone reaches such a state, it becomes clear what evils they will be capable of committing. At the same time, reformation will also be very difficult because such individuals are past caring about themselves and they are no longer concerned with improving their behavior.

[82] *Biḥār al-Anwār*, Vol. 74, P. 147.

The Real Eid—A True Day of Celebration

Imām ʿAlī has said:

Indeed, this day is Eid for those whose fasting is accepted by Allah, and whose prayers He is pleased with; and (in fact) every day that a sin is not committed against Allah is an Eid (a day of celebration).[83]

Eid al-Fiṭr, the celebration that we hold after fasting during the blessed month of Ramaḍān, is in reality a celebration over our conquest of our lusts and desires. This is a celebration of our obedience to Allah and His commands. Therefore, such a day is a day of celebration for those who obeyed Allah in His commands and understood the ultimate philosophy of their actions. Yet for those who dishonored such a month and did not attempt to educate and train themselves in the obedience of Allah, such a day will be nothing but a day of grief and sorrow.

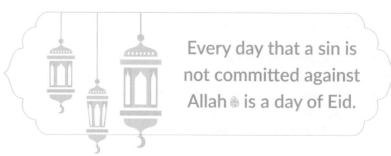

Every day that a sin is not committed against Allah is a day of Eid.

[83] *Nahj al-Balāghah*, Short Saying 428.

Valuable Investments

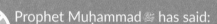

Prophet Muḥammad ﷺ has said:

Allah ﷻ does not look at your faces or your wealth; rather, He looks at your hearts and your actions.[84]

Even though most societies judge people based on how they look and how much money they have, Islam explicitly mentions that such judgments are actually incorrect and misguided. What Allah ﷻ really judges is our hearts (meaning our intentions and beliefs) and our actions. Our hearts are the root of all of our actions and if we possess pure hearts, then likewise, our actions will be pure and wholesome as well. In front of Allah's judgment, the only successful people are those who possess these valuable things.

[84] *Al-Maḥajjat al-Bayḍā'*, Vol. 6, P. 312.

LESSON EIGHTY-FOUR

Two Things which Cause People's Destruction

Imām ʿAlī ﷺ has said:

Two things have thrown people into destruction, and these are the fear of poverty and the seeking of glory.[85]

There are two things which are the root causes for the increase that we see in theft, bribery, and various other crimes in our society, and these are: the fear of poverty and the seeking of glory. Similarly, if we look at the root causes of greed and the accumulation of wealth in various individuals, we find that such behavior is also caused by these same two factors.

When we look at some people, we find that in spite of the great amount of wealth that they possess, they are still engaged in the continuous accumulation of more material wealth. In some cases, they even break laws for fear of somehow losing their wealth and becoming poverty stricken; this is in spite of possessing millions or even billions of dollars in their bank accounts. In other cases, people give up their sense of peace and calm in order to seek ever-increasing levels of glory and social recognition. They do this so that they can compete with their rivals and show themselves as being superior. However, if they were to give up these two negative traits, then their lives would be filled with ease and happiness.

[85] *Tuḥaf al-ʿUqūl.*

LESSON EIGHTY-FIVE

Do Not Count Such Works as Being Little!

Imām as-Sajjād ﷺ has said:

Actions which are based on sincerity and piety are never small, even if they outwardly appear to be so. How is it possible that an action accepted by Allah ﷻ could be small (in nature)?[86]

The Qur'ān states: "Allah only accepts those actions which are accompanied by piety and pure intentions." Therefore, we should pay close attention to the purity of our intentions, our sincerity, and our God-consciousness when it comes to our actions and not just their quantity. This is because no matter how small our actions may be, if they are done with sincerity and piety, then they are of great value before Allah ﷻ and considered an action that is accepted by Him. Can an action accepted by Allah ﷻ ever be considered as small? In conclusion, the actions which are based on insincerity and showing off are those that are without value, and those which are based on sincerity of intention and piety are valuable and weighty in front of Allah ﷻ.

---

[86] *Tuḥaf al-'Uqūl*, P. 201.

Mistakes, Misdeeds, and Apologies

Imām Ḥusayn has said:

Do not perform bad actions, for then, apologizing will be an inevitable consequence. This is because a believing person does not perform evil deeds such that they have to apologize later (as a consequence of their bad actions). However, a hypocrite performs bad actions and seeks pardon every day.[87]

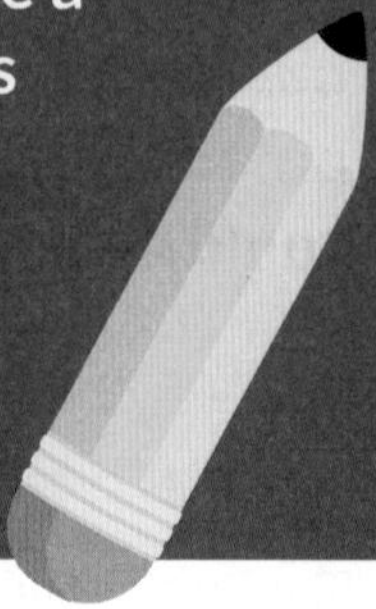

Every individual makes mistakes, but people of faith and hypocrites have a critical difference in this regard. Believers strive to make less mistakes and apologize less because they realize that apologizing is only a second best. One of the marks of believers is that they quickly learn and do not keep repeating their mistakes; this is also in line with the issue of faith where one's inner reality is the same as their outer reality.

If they are pure internally, then this will reflect clearly on their behavior.

[87] *Tuḥaf al-'Uqūl*, P. 177.

The Worst Way of Living

Imām ar-Riḍā ﷺ has said:

The worst of the people in respect to their economic lives are those who do not help others with their livelihood...[88]

One of the worst attributes in a human being is the attribute of greed and miserliness. Sometimes, people fall into the trap of thinking that if they hoard their wealth and keep it all for themselves, they will gain a stronger position in terms of power and wealth in this world. They refuse to help others, even their close family members. This type of greed and miserliness comes from a lack of understanding that wealth has no intrinsic value in and of itself—its value comes from the benefit that it provides to oneself and others. Such people have failed to understand the purpose of this life, and the reason behind why Allah ﷻ has given them wealth.

[88] *Tuḥaf al-'Uqūl*, P. 334.

LESSON EIGHTY-EIGHT

Our Promise is Our Debt

Imām ar-Riḍā ﷺ has said:

We are a family who considers our promises to be just like our debts, and this is how the Prophet of Allah ﷺ was.[89]

Debts are not only when we borrow something from others and then are indebted to them as a result of that. Those who make a promise to someone are in reality in their debt, and they are responsible to fulfill their moral and ethical obligations toward them. This is something which cannot simply be shrugged off.

Being loyal to one's word is a sign of character, faith, and truthfulness; and it also helps to solidify the bonds of trust within a society. It is something which strengthens the spirit of social cooperation, and it is for these reasons that Islam has placed great importance on fulfilling one's promises.

[89] *Tuḥaf al-ʿUqūl*, P. 333.

LESSON EIGHTY-NINE

The Property of the People

Imām al-Bāqir ﷺ has said:

Whenever an individual takes in wealth through unlawful means, neither their Ḥajj nor ʿUmrah (pilgrimage), nor their actions to strengthen family relationships will be accepted.[90]

Good intentions by themselves are not enough in Islam. What is further necessary is the purity of the means through which we perform these righteous deeds. Those who perform good actions through illegitimate means will never reach their end goals. Until the means are as pure as the intentions behind them, neither of them will be accepted by Allah ﷻ.

[90] *Safīnat al-Biḥār*, Vol. 1, P. 213.

LESSON NINETY

Do Not Seek Things from People as Much as Possible

Imām as-Sajjād ‎ has said:

Requesting things from other people is (a kind) of abjectness in life which will destroy one's humility and weaken one's character and standing. It is a (type of) poverty that people create for themselves.[91]

Some people throw themselves into poverty as a result of actions which they believe will actually save them from it. They request things from people which are not necessary and in turn make themselves dependent and needy upon them. Through such behavior, their character is weakened and ruined in front of others. Islam has ordered its followers to stand upon their own two feet as much as possible and be wary of dependence in their lives. This is because taking care of one's needs through others is the worst type of neediness and poverty.

[91] *Tuḥaf al-'Uqūl*, P. 201.

Woe Upon Such a Person

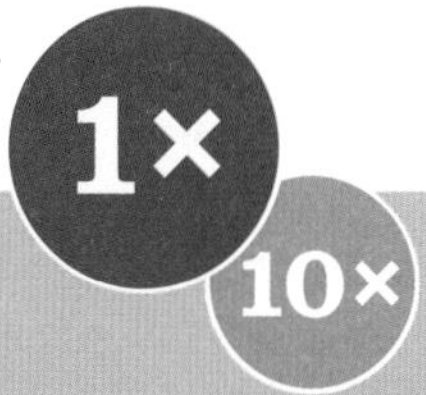

Imām as-Sajjād ﷺ has said:

Woe upon those people whose ones exceed their tens![92]

Allah ﷻ says in the Qur'ān:

Whoever brings virtue shall receive ten times its like; but whoever brings vice shall not be requited except with its like...[93]

This tradition mentions that the truly wretched are those whose tens (good deeds which are rewarded ten times as much) are exceeded by their ones (bad deeds which are only punished one for one—not multiplied like the good deeds). Imagine that Allah ﷻ is rewarding you ten times for the good you have done and only punishing you to the degree of the sins, but in spite of this, the good is still outweighed by the bad. This is truly the ultimate disgrace and wretchedness.

[92] *Tuḥaf al-'Uqūl*, P. 203.
[93] Sūrah al-An'ām (6), Verse 160.

LESSON NINETY-TWO

Do Not Attempt to Resolve Your Problems through the Commission of Sins

Imām Ḥusayn has said:

A person who seeks to do something through sinning against Allah will lose what one hopes for sooner and reach what one feared more quickly.[94]

Some people think that they will reach their goals sooner if they resort to unlawful (ḥarām) means. For example, someone may be in a financial bind and may think that by opening up a liquor store, they can save themselves from their financial problems and gain significant amounts of profit. However, this tradition explicitly mentions that this is not the case, and in fact they will become even further engulfed in various issues than they were in before.

In other cases, some people may think that because they are constantly suffering from financial issues, once they make more money, they can finally gain a sense of inner peace and calm. They anticipate that the quickest way to make this money will be through various unlawful means. However, after making lots of money, they realize that they have not gained any additional sense of peace, and in fact are more stressed out and anxious than ever before. This shows that people should never seek what they need through unlawful means as such actions will only take them further away from their goals.

[94] *Tuḥaf al-'Uqūl*, P. 977.

Those Who are Satisfied with Themselves

Imām ʿAlī has said:

One who is self-satisfied and egotistic will have many (people) who are not happy with them.[95]

Although having love for oneself and confidence at a moderate level is necessary for the continuation of life, it is possible that people exceed these normal boundaries and reach a point of selfishness or egotism. Those people who are egotistical never see their own personal faults and consider themselves to be pure, without any faults, and loveable all at the same time. They believe they are the cream of the crop in their society and the best at everything they do. For this same reason, they have great expectations from other people and this can cause individuals to resent and eventually hate them.

[95] *Nahj al-Balāghah*, Short Saying 6.

Close and Far Relatives

Imām Ḥasan al-Mujtabā has said:

One's close relatives are those who have the most love for you, even if they are far in lineage; and the far relatives are those who have less love and affection for you, even if they are from your close relatives.[96]

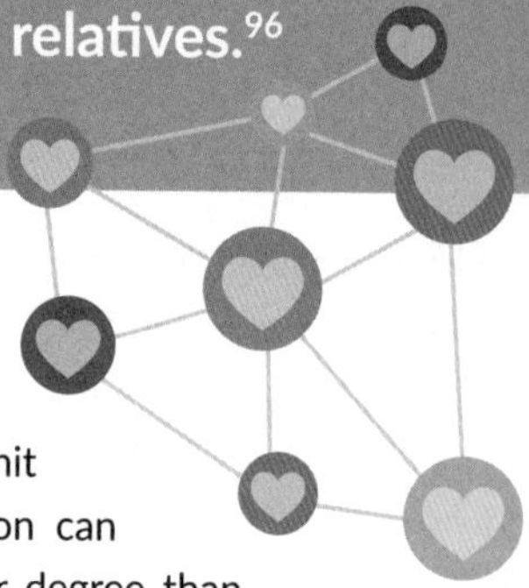

The relationship between relatives is one of the most important social institutions in Islam. Such relationships are comprised of tighter knit groups in the society where cooperation can extend to a higher and greater degree than in the society overall. This relationship is instrumental in the resolution of problems that come up from time to time. This tradition emphasizes that these relationships must in reality be based on love and affection, and not only on simple lineage and family blood.

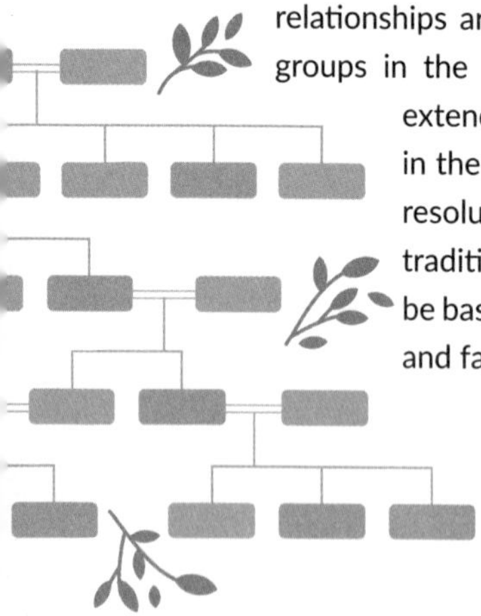

[96] *Tuḥaf al-'Uqūl*, P. 165.

LESSON NINETY-FIVE

Breaking Bad Habits

Imām Ḥasan al-ʿAskarī has said:

Breaking people's incorrect habits is something like a miracle.[97]

Upholding certain (good) habits are actually one of the great Divine blessings because it can make difficult things easier for people to perform. Many of the complex tasks which we must do in our day to day lives are made automatic through their habitual nature. At the same time, bad habits can also become engrained and automatic in nature. When a negative behavior becomes enshrined in habit, it will be very dangerous and eliminating it from our lives can be a very difficult task. Imām al-ʿAskarī has considered the breaking of such bad habits to be similar in nature to a miracle.

We should strive not to cultivate negative habits to begin with so we avoid the very difficult and time-consuming task of breaking them later on in our lives.

[97] *Biḥār al-Anwār*, Vol. 17, P. 217.

LESSON NINETY-SIX

The Tragedy of Karbalāʾ

Imām Ḥusayn ﷺ has said:

I swear by Allah ﷻ that I will never put my hand in theirs[98] like an abject person, nor will I run away like a slave... I see death as nothing but felicity, and life with the oppressors as nothing but the cause of misery and affliction.[99]

Live and die with honor and dignity

The day of ʿĀshūrāʾ will never be forgotten, and it can be considered as a great university for all of humankind. There are many lessons that can be learned by all people who wish to live and die with honor and dignity. The lessons taught to us on that day can fill volumes with its wisdom. The aforementioned lines from Imām Ḥusayn ﷺ are but a small indication of who he was and how he lived his life. If we study his life and actions on that momentous day, surely we too will be able to live and die with full honor and dignity.

[98] In order to pledge allegiance to Yazīd.
[99] *Maqtal al-Ḥusayn*, Pp. 246 and 256.

LESSON NINETY-SEVEN

Who is the Intelligent One?

Imām ʿAlī ﷺ was asked to describe the signs of someone who is intelligent. He replied by saying:

An intelligent person is the one who places everything in its proper place.[100]

There is much that has been said in regards to what intelligence actually is—out of all of what has been said, this short tradition above is the best description of what intelligence truly is. Intelligence is nothing but the placement of all things in their proper place. An intelligent individual will place happiness and sorrow, friendship and enmity, mildness and harshness, affection, worship, work, leisure, and all other things in their proper place. When all of these things are positioned corrrectly, then that individual will truly be one who is the epitome of intelligence.

[100] *Nahj al-Balāghah*, Short Saying 235.

LESSON NINETY-EIGHT

The Cause of Enmity

Imām ʿAlī has said:

People are enemies of what they do not know.[101]

We see that some people reject certain things and they stand up against them in opposition. One of the reasons for their opposition is because they do not understand them or it is something new to them. This wise saying is particularly true in regards to religious matters. Some people easily reject religious matters when they do not understand them and this applies even to those who are learned in other fields. You would think that someone who has taken the time to learn another field would understand that it takes much work in order to master a given subject, and therefore they should not be so quick to judge something which they do not comprehend in regards to a certain other matter.

Therefore, we should be careful never to reject something simply because it may seem strange to us or because we do not understand it.

[101] *Nahj al-Balāghah*, Short Saying 172.

The Ones who Possesses Ghayrah[102]

Prophet Muḥammad ﷺ has said:

Allah ﷻ, the Almighty, loves those of His servants who are Ghayūr.[103]

Ghayrah is in reality a sense of loyalty and protectiveness over one's religion and family. It can even extend to wanting to protect one's country as well. A Ghayūr individual feels responsible toward protecting these things and becomes extremely upset when a stranger encroaches upon them. Ghayrah is one of the prominent characteristics of the Prophets ﷺ and the people of Allah ﷻ. Ghayrah is critical to protect oneself, as well as one's religion, family, and people against attacks by outsiders.

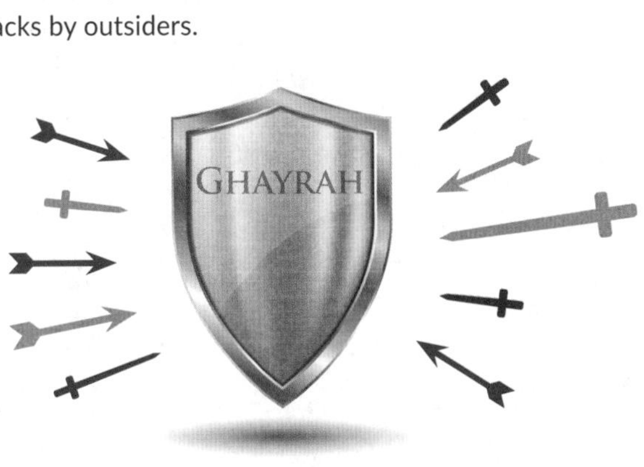

[102] This term refers to those who have a protective sense toward their religion, their people, and their family. An individual who possesses this feeling of protectiveness is called Ghayūr.

[103] *Nahj al-Faṣāḥah*, P. 15.

A Blessed Existence

Prophet Muḥammad ﷺ has said:

A believing individual is much like a date tree. Everything that comes from it is beneficial and advantageous.[104]

The date palm is a tree that is full of advantageous uses and blessings. We are able to eat from its fruit, which is considered to be one of the healthiest and most nutritious fruits on this planet. Its seeds can be used as fuel for fire, and its palm fronds can be woven into mats, hats, and table covers. Its wood can be used in buildings, as well as in the construction of bridges. Even its blossoms can be used in fragrant perfumes, thus every single part of the palm tree has a use and the tree in its entirety is of great blessings for all of humanity.

People who have faith are similar to this tree when it comes to their benefits. Their thoughts, their words, their gatherings, their friendship, their decision-making, and in reality everything which comes from them is blessed and helps people.

Everything they do or say is full of advantage and blessing for their society.

[104] *Nahj al-Faṣāḥah*, P. 564.

The Best of Hands

Prophet Muḥammad ﷺ has said:

There are three kinds of hands—the hand which takes, the hand which remains, and the hand which gives; and the best of hands are the hands that give.[105]

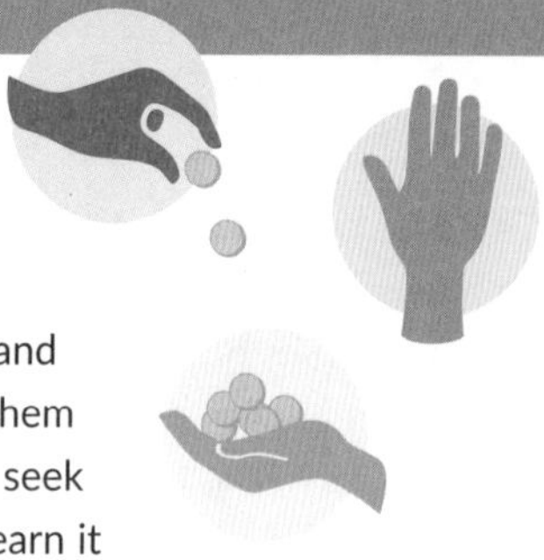

Islam has always encouraged its followers to do their best and work hard in life. This extends not only to the physical and material, but the spiritual and emotional apects as well. In addition, it has taught them to be independent as much as possible and not seek things from other people when they can work and earn it themselves. Not only does the religion ask that they not seek things from others, but it recommends that they put themselves in a position where they are the ones who are giving back to others.

This tradition establishes a concept that the best of hands are those which give to others, and not those which only take from other people.

[105] *Tuḥaf al-ʿUqūl*, P. 32.

LESSON ONE HUNDRED AND TWO

Worse than Death

Imām Ḥasan al-ʿAskarī has said:

Better than life is that thing which if you lose it you become disgusted with life, and worse than death is that thing which if it comes to you makes you love death.[106]

Some people imagine that the most valuable things in this world are found in those things which relate to the material, however there are a multitude of things much greater in value. There are non-material things, which if lost, will cause unbelievable anguish to a person. These are things which no amount of money or wealth can replace or make up for. We should always be careful to keep things in perspective and be thankful for the multitude of blessings which Allah has given to us.

[106] *Tuḥaf al-ʿUqūl*, P. 368.

The Difference Between a Believer and a Hypocrite

Prophet Muḥammad ﷺ has said:

Whenever you see a believing individual engrossed in silence, then draw near them for you will hear words full of wisdom. Faithful individuals are of few words but much action, while the hypocrites are of many words but few actions.[107]

Human beings have a finite amount of energy, and it is for this reason that when they expend much of their energy toward a specific task, they will find themselves limited in what they can do in regards to other things in their lives. Therefore, it is not surprising that people who speak too much often fall short when it comes to their actions.

The Prophet of Islam ﷺ described the people of faith as those who are filled with the spirit of hard work, rather than the spirit of talkativeness. Hypocrites, on the other hand, are devoid of the spirit of faith and spend their time talking instead of working. We should always strive to be like those whom the Prophet ﷺ has described as believers and not those who are hypocrites.

[107] *Tuḥaf al-'Uqūl*, P. 296.

The Best Inheritance

Imām ʿAlī has said:

The best thing which parents can leave behind for their children is good behavior.[108]

Good behavior is defined by the positive way that we interact with others, and the respect and generosity of spirit that we show to them. In some cases, good behavior is exhibited in front of Allah's creation; while in other cases, it is exhibited in front of Allah Himself. In both cases, it is one of the greatest resources which human beings possess and it is the key to their success in all aspects of life.

For this same reason, Imām ʿAlī mentions that the greatest inheritance which parents can leave for their children is good behavior. Many times, parents think that the best inheritance they can leave behind is found in materialistic things such as big homes and large bank accounts, and they end up neglecting everything else. However, good behavior is the root of love, ease in living, friendship, and even unity amongst people. It is an important factor in how effective our speech is, and how well we are able to progress in our social lives. There is no doubt that good character and manners is the best inheritance which parents can leave for their children.

108 *Ghurar al-Ḥikam*, P. 393.

LESSON ONE HUNDRED AND FIVE

Respecting Freedom of Thought

Prophet Muḥammad ﷺ has said:

When a believing individual is forced to hide one's beliefs and live in a hidden manner amongst a group of people, those are truly bad people.[109]

When a person is forced to hide one's true beliefs and is not able to speak or practice freely, then this is a sign that a selfish majority has forced their views on others which in turn is preventing the minority from expressing their thoughts and beliefs. There is no doubt that such a society will not be able to reach felicity. Righteous people who live in a healthy society must always be given the right to practice their beliefs and express their thoughts as they wish. If they comprise a minority in that society, then the majority should never prevent them from living in this manner. Their rights must be respected and they should be left free to propagate the truth.

[109] *Nahj al-Faṣāḥah.*

Six Characteristics Which are Not Present in True Believers

Imām aṣ-Ṣādiq ﷺ has said:

There are six things which must not exist in a believing individual: severity, ill-manners, jealousy, stubbornness, lying, and oppression.[110]

People who consider themselves as believers are potentially fooling themselves if they possess certain attributes and characteristics. At the very least, true believers should be free from the six negative attributes which have been mentioned in this tradition. What is interesting is that these six characteristics are all connected to how people relate to one another socially. The true believers are those who are easy going, good-natured, benevolent, and submit to the truth. They are furthermore truthful, just, and justice seeking for others. The title of a believer is an extremely high-ranking status that is not suitable for those who possess any of the six attributes mentioned above.

We should judge ourselves first and foremost, and see if we possess any of these six negative attributes.

[110] *Tuḥaf al-'Uqūl*, P. 282.

severity

ill-manners

jealousy

stubbornness

lying

oppression

LESSON ONE HUNDRED AND SEVEN

Be Careful of Your Duties Toward Allah

Imām aṣ-Ṣādiq has said:

Be careful of (your duties to) Allah and sanctify Him even if it is only a little. Place a curtain between Him and yourself even if it is very thin.[111]

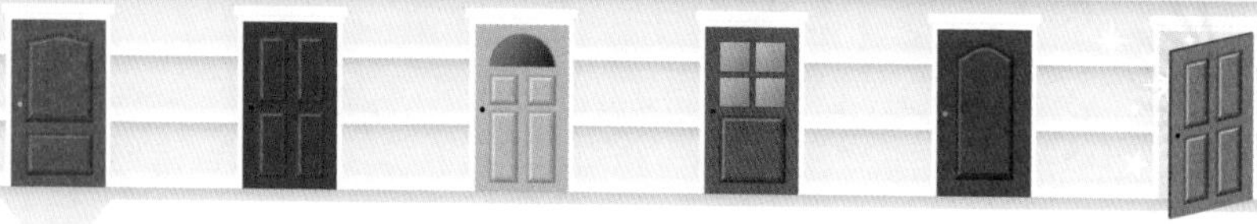

When people walk on the path of sin, they quickly cut off their previous connections with Allah. They burn their bridges and they shut the doors which would make their return possible. In this tradition, Imām aṣ-Ṣādiq is saying that such people should at least leave one door open. One day, such individuals will naturally feel regret for their actions and if they have left this one door open, then they can have a means of return.

111 *Tuḥaf al-'Uqūl*, P. 268.

True Worship

Imām ʿAlī is narrated to have said to Kumayl:

O Kumayl, it is not important that you simply pray, fast, and give in the way of Allah. What is important is that your prayers are performed with a pure heart, that your actions are done for the pleasure of Allah and that they are performed with humility.[112]

The real value of our actions is not based on how many times we do them, but the quality that they are done with. It is the inner reality of worship which is important and not just its outer manifestations. In this tradition, Imām ʿAlī was emphasizing to Kumayl that simply sufficing with the outer aspects of worship and their quantity is not enough; rather, it is necessary for one to go to the heart of the matter. It is this inner reality which will help us to grow and reach human completion. We should always keep this point in mind and attempt to perform our acts of worship with the purest of intentions and the utmost level of care.

[112] *Tuḥaf al-ʿUqūl*, P. 117.

Do Not Forget Your Defects!

Imām aṣ-Ṣādiq ﷺ has said:

When a person seeks out the sins of others and criticizes them, but at the same time forgets one's own sins, then know that they will be entangled in Divine punishment.[113]

There are many people who are quite brazen in criticizing others and pointing out their faults, but at the same time, they are completely negligent of their own negative characteristics and traits. They criticize others for their small faults yet ignore their own major shortcomings. Such people are afflicted with selfishness and egoism due to the veils of arrogance and unawareness which have covered their eyes from seeing their own reality.

A superior individual tries to remove one's own defects before looking at the defects of others.

[113] *Tuḥaf al-'Uqūl*, P. 271.

LESSON ONE HUNDRED AND TEN

The Great Torture

Imām aṣ-Ṣādiq ﷺ has said:

One who is ill-mannered torments oneself.[114]

It is commonly understood that people who have a bad attitude and are always ill-mannered toward others are a cause of their friends and close relatives' torment. By associating with such a person, they undergo various hardships and difficulties due to their negative behavior. While this is undoubtedly correct, such people are actually a source of the greatest torment for themselves and their entire lives are made bitter and unlivable as a result. Such negative and pessimistic people usually live shorter lives, and they spend their days upset at everything and everyone.

Contrary to this is someone who has good behavior and sees life in a positive light. This type of demeanor and viewpoint is actually considered to be a form of great worship by the religion of Islam and it has been emphasized and encouraged. It is counted as one of the important factors which will allow us to enter into Paradise.

[114] *Tuḥaf al-'Uqūl*, P. 270.

القرآن الكريم

The Vitality and Freshness of the Qur'ān

Imām ar-Riḍā ﷺ has said:

Allah ﷻ did not make the Qur'ān for a specific time period, nor for a specified group of people. Therefore, it is new and fresh during every time period, and for every group (of people) until the Day of Judgment.[115]

The Imām ﷺ mentioned these words when someone asked him why the Qur'ān never gets old, even after countless recitations. The Imām ﷺ pointed out the reality that the Qur'ān was not created in this world, which is oft-changing and in constant flux. It is a Book which is rooted in Allah's lofty knowledge, so it is of an eternal nature. When something is of an eternal nature, then whatever comes from it will always be fresh and captivating. Indeed, this is one of the signs of the greatness and high status of the Qur'ān.

[115] *Safinat al-Biḥār*, Vol. 2, P. 413.

Be Cautious of Worshiping Your Desires

Imām aṣ-Ṣādiq ﷺ has said:

Fear your passions and desires just as you fear your diehard enemies, for there is no enemy that can be worse for a person than following one's desires...[116]

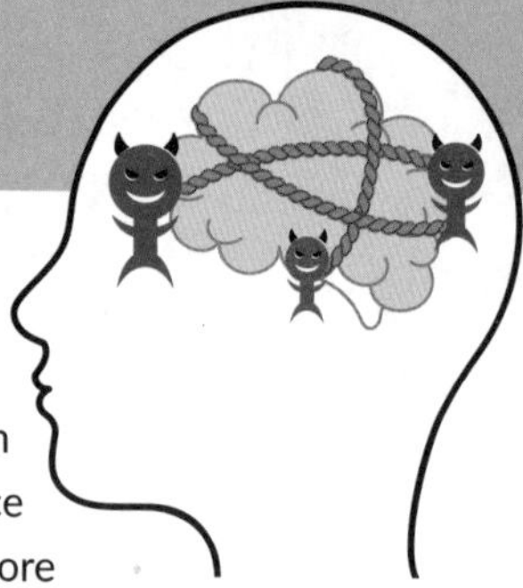

There is no doubt that internal enemies are more dangerous than external enemies. It is for this reason that our rebellious passions and desires, which influence us from the darkest recesses of our hearts, are more dangerous than any other enemy we can possibly face. The worship of these dark desires blind the eyes and seal the ears of the people; they shut down the proper functioning of the intellect and make us unable to see the true realities. As a result of this, such a person will be thrown into the depths of deviation and corruption.

[116] *Safīnat al-Biḥār*, Vol. 2, root word Hawā.

Being a True Follower of the Ahl al-Bayt

Imām al-Bāqir is narrated to have said to Jābir ibn Juʿfī:

Send my greetings to my Shīʿahs and tell them that there is no kinship between us and Allah, but the only way to gain nearness to Him is through obeying His commands. [117 & 118]

There are many people who think that by just calling themselves Shīʿahs or by having love toward the family of the Prophet, this will somehow save them from any level of accountability for their actions. They believe that by simply saying that they love the Ahl al-Bayt, they will be counted among their followers. They furthermore think that since the Imāms and the Ahl al-Bayt are close to Allah, they will use their influence to save them. However, the relationship between Allah and His creations is based on following and obeying His commands.

Whoever obeys Allah's commands the most will be the closest to Him, and whoever commits the most sins will be the furthest from Him, no matter who they are.

[117] This tradition is referring to the fact that the Imāms have a special link with Allah due to their merits, and their closeness to Allah is based on their obedience to Him. Similarly, our relationship with Allah can be strengthened by obeying His commands.

[118] *Biḥār al-Anwār*, Vol. 15, P. 164.

Relationship Between Wealth and its Consumption

Imām ʿAlī has said:

A person who gains wealth through unlawful means will spend that wealth in a way which will entail no divine reward.[119]

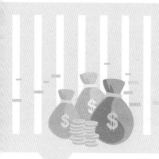

People often say that not just any money is worthy of being spent in positive ways, and if someone wants to spend money toward good, then that money should first have been obtained through pure and lawful ways. This tradition shows the veracity of this common saying. How can people think that they can spend unlawfully gained wealth and somehow attain positive results for themselves? How can any reward be expected when the source of that money was unlawful to begin with?

Such money may even end up having consequences that are completely opposite to what was originally intended. On the other hand, even a small amount of money gained in lawful ways, will end up having tremendous positive effects. Therefore, one must always keep in mind that the root of money and the way through which it is earned have an effect both on the end result, as well as the reward which will be given for such actions.

[119] *Tuḥaf al-ʿUqūl*, P. 63.

The Most Truthful and the Most Learned

Prophet Muḥammad ﷺ has said:

Every nation has its Ṣiddīq and Farūq,[120] and the Ṣiddīq and Farūq of this nation is ʿAlī ibn Abī Ṭālib عليه السلام.[121]

In order to implement and organize a proper and cohesive religious society, it was necessary for there to be someone who was capable to lead the people after the passing away of the Prophet of Islam ﷺ. The Prophet ﷺ spent many years engaged in building the very basic foundations of an Islamic society. Much time had also been spent fighting against the polytheists and other enemies of the new faith.

Someone worthy and befitting was necessary to continue this building process and to distinguish between the truth and falsehood (in essence, someone who was a Farūq). Someone was also necessary who could explain the realities of Islam appropriately and clearly (one who was a Ṣiddīq) so that all of the questions of the people could be answered properly. The only person who was worthy of such a role was ʿAlī ibn Abī Ṭālib عليه السلام, and no one else in the entire community was capable of fulfilling such a position.

[120] The term Ṣiddīq can be understood to mean 'a truthful individual,' and the term Farūq can be understood as 'one who discerns and distinguishes between truth and falsehood.'

[121] *Safīnat al-Biḥār*, Vol. 2, P. 221.

Simple Living and Cooperation in Home Life

Imām aṣ-Ṣādiq has said:

ʿAlī would bring firewood from the desert, bring water, and clean; while Fāṭimah would make flour, knead the dough, and bake the bread.[122]

This tradition is a small glimpse into the lives of Imām ʿAlī and Lady Fāṭimah and how they would conduct their day to day affairs. They lived their lives with the utmost simplicity and without any excess or waste. Their lives were filled with happiness, affection, cooperation, and vitality. Work was not seen as something to be shied away from, and mutual support and understanding were seen as a foundation of life. Unfortunately, in most cases these are things which have been lost in modern day life and along with them, we have also lost much of our day to day peace and tranquility.

[122] *Safīnat al-Biḥār*, Vol. 2, P. 195.

One Hour of Justice

Prophet Muḥammad ﷺ has said:

One hour of (the implementation of) justice is better than a year of worship.[123]

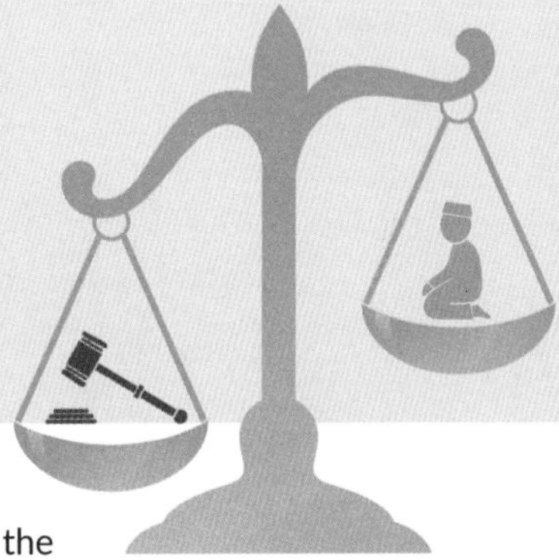

Worship is a connection between the Creator and the created, and understanding this relationship holds many inner lessons for us and it brings about the growth and progression of the human intellect and spirit. In spite of the importance that worship holds, the tradition above surprisingly says that one hour where justice is implemented is superior to one year of optional worship. The question comes up as to how such a thing is possible?

In other traditions, we also see how one hour of contemplation and thought are superior to one whole night (or according to other narrations, one whole year's worship). Such traditions teach us how important justice (as well as thinking and contemplation) are in Allah's eyes. What is interesting to note is that both contemplation and justice have common roots, meaning that where there is no justice, there can also be no thought or contemplation.

[123] *Nahj al-Faṣāḥah*, P. 410.

The True Doctor

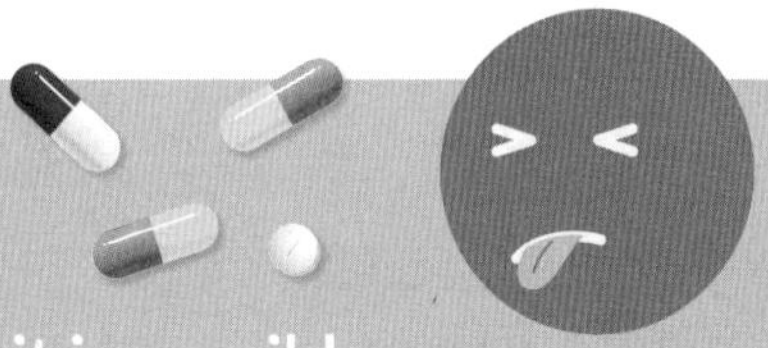

Prophet Muḥammad ﷺ has said:

The true physician is Allah ﷻ and it is possible that there are some things which are beneficial for you but others see them as being harmful.[124]

In some cases, many of the difficulties that people face in their lives are caused by a lack of proper thinking or a lack of proper choice. In other situations, people are faced with certain undesirable events which are not caused by their own choices and they become needful of a 'physician' who can cure them. One must be aware though that the master physician is none other than Allah ﷻ who possesses powerful types of medicine which can completely cure His ill patients. Sometimes, these medicines can be quite bitter and difficult to take, but they have powerful and beneficial effects on the diseases which people are suffering from.

In all cases, Allah ﷻ is the master physician, and even though His medicine may initially be difficult to take, He is All-Aware of how best to cure His patients.

---

[124] *Nahj al-Faṣāḥah*, P. 406.

The Successors of the Prophet ﷺ

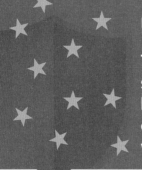

Prophet Muḥammad ﷺ has said:

This religion will always be eminent and safe (from the hands of the enemies) because of the 12 (individuals who will come after the Prophet ﷺ), all of whom will be from the Quraysh.[125]

Many of the most accepted books of the Ahl as-Sunnah have mentioned similar traditions in regards to the 12 leaders. These books include: *Ṣaḥīḥ al-Bukhārī*, *Ṣaḥīḥ Muslim*, *Sunan at-Tirmidhī*, *Sunan Abī Dāwūd*, *Musnad Aḥmad ibn Ḥanbal*, as well as many others. These narrations number around 271 when we count all of the Shīʿah and Sunnī sources through which they have been narrated. What is even more interesting is that these 12 guides cannot correspond to anything other than the 12 Shīʿah Imāms ؑ when we look at the entirety of Islamic history.

When we look at the first three Caliphs, or the Caliphs of the Umayyads and Abbasids, none of them can be found to be amongst these 12 who have been mentioned. Due to this reason, the scholars of the Ahl as-Sunnah have faced great difficulty in trying to decipher and categorize who these 12 actually are. However, the Shīʿahs easily understand who these traditions are referring to and are clearly able to identify who these 12 leaders are.[126]

125 *Taysīr al-Wuṣūl*

126 See P. 192 for the names of these 12 leaders as mentioned by Prophet Muḥammad ﷺ.

A Gathering of Sin

Imām aṣ-Ṣādiq ﷺ has said:

It is not worthy of the believers to sit in a gathering where there are sins (taking place) if they are not able to stop them.[127]

Participating in a gathering of sin is a sin in itself even if the individual does not partake in the sinning, and one does not become like the people of that gathering. This is because being part of such a gathering is the same as approving that sin, unless an individual has the intention of stopping them or transforming the gathering into one which is positive and where good will be performed. This is actually a major responsibility in Islam and it is known as 'commanding the good and forbidding the evil.' When a person looks at something that is sinful while being indifferent toward what is happening, it will create a spirit within them where the ugliness of that sin will become lessened, and the individual will slowly become accustomed to the performance of that sin.

[127] *Uṣūl al-Kāfī*, Vol. 2, P. 374.

Engage in Works of Agriculture

Imām aṣ-Ṣādiq ﷺ has said:

Engage in agriculture and the planting of trees, for I swear by Allah ﷻ that people can not perform purer or more lawful (ḥalāl) work than this.[128]

Farming is one of the foundational aspects which human life is based upon and much of what people in society do would be impossible without it. Industrial factories and businesses would be unsustainable without established agriculture and farming, and this is because without the raw products provided by agriculture, factories and businesses would not have the base products necessary for their work. Another interesting aspect of farming is that while it is possible to cheat and adulterate when it comes to other lines of work, such a thing is not possible when it comes to farming. At the end of the day, fruit is fruit and only so much can be done with it. Farmers must also work hard and their work is honest work; it is for this reason that the above tradition considers agriculture as being one of the most wholesome and pure lines of work that can be performed.

---

[128] *Safīnat al-Biḥār*, Vol. 1, P. 549.

LESSON ONE HUNDRED AND TWENTY-TWO

The Duration of Life

Imām 'Alī ﷺ has said:

Death which arrives earlier for human beings as a result of sins is more common than death which comes as a result of their natural lifespan; and the extended lifespan of people as a result of their good deeds is more common than their actual natural life spans.[129]

It is clear that various sins are known to directly affect the length of our lives in a negative fashion. Things such as drinking alcohol, gambling, miserliness, and envy are known to have a negative effect on one's lifespan. In addition to these sins, there are other things which exert an indirect effect on the duration of one's life. These indirect factors work through destabilizing the society, destroying public safety and security, and bringing about conflict and wars—and these include things like usury and oppression.

At the same time, positive actions have their own deep effects on the calm and tranquility that people feel within their souls and their conscience, and this affects the length of their life spans in a positive manner. Therefore, we should realize that sins not only have spiritual effects, but they certainly have physical effects as well. These physical effects can go as far as affecting the quality of our physical lives, as well as how long we will live.

[129] *Safīnat al-Biḥār*, P. 489.

Cooperation with Satan

Imām ʿAlī ﷺ has said:

Do not curse Satan openly while you are his friend in secret.[130]

Many people express hatred for things like poverty or hypocrisy, while others will express hatred for figures such as Satan, who is an avowed enemy of humankind. While they express such hatred outwardly, they are practically engulfed in the very same things they profess to hate. For example, there are some extremely wealthy individuals who fear poverty to such a degree that they live their lives just like the poverty stricken; and they are terrified of spending any money so they deprive themselves of everything in life.

Similarly, there are some hypocrites who are constantly busy speaking against hypocrisy, yet they themselves are engulfed in hypocrisy from head to toe. There are others who are greatly influenced by Satan and follow him, yet they constantly express negative views in regards to him. This is while they openly do what Allah ﷻ has made unlawful and easily allow themselves to be influenced and controlled by Satan himself. Therefore, people should be aware that it is not enough to simply express an idea or concept outwardly, rather they must internally manifest that concept as well.

[130] *Turāth al-Aʾimmah*, P. 209.

LESSON ONE HUNDRED AND TWENTY-FOUR

Consult with Others so that You May be Guided

Imām Ḥasan al-Mujtabā ﷺ has said:

No group consulted with one another in their works but that they were guided to their best interests.[131]

When people cooperate and work with one another, this becomes a source of goodness and great blessings for them. They progress and are able to do things which would have been impossible for them individually. This is particularly true when it comes to intellectual and organizational issues, where the combined ideas of many people will have an especially powerful effect. Some individuals are unfortunately affected by a sense of stubbornness when it comes to the issue of consultation, so they refuse to seek the advice of others.

Such people will find themselves constantly making mistakes and being entangled in various problems. The reason behind this is that each individual is able to see only one facet of an issue (or at the very most, several facets). It is very rare to find someone who is able to look at an issue from all of the possible angles. Therefore, when people consult others, they are able to better understand a given issue and this will aid them in making a more comprehensive decision. Such decisions will almost always be stronger and more correct than a decision made by someone who can only see one side of the issue. Let us make a firm decision to always consult others during appropriate circumstances for this is the way to success and proper decision making in life.

[131] *Tuḥaf al-'Uqūl*, P. 164.

LESSON ONE HUNDRED AND TWENTY-FIVE

Greet One Another with Salām

Imām Ḥusayn has said:

The (greeting of) Salām has 70 rewards—of which 69 of them are for the initiator of the greeting, while 1 of them is for the one who responds.[132]

Amongst all of the greetings that people around the world give to one another, the Islamic greeting (which is Salāmun ʿalaykum—meaning peace be upon you) has a particularly special context and meaning. This is because it is both a welcoming greeting, as well as a sign of peace, happiness, and friendship. At the same time, it also conveys a positive desire for the person's health and soundness (physical, mental, and spiritual). It is for this reason that the greetings of the dwellers of Paradise will be this same Salām. In addition, the angels will also greet the people who have lived pure lives with this greeting.

Unfortunately, some people among the Muslims believe that initiating this greeting or replying to it is actually a sign of weakness. They therefore abstain from greeting others or even replying to their greeting. What they do not understand is that by not addressing others in this way, they are missing out on a great blessing, and this above tradition explains how great the rewards are for such an action.

[132] *Tuḥaf al-ʿUqūl*, P. 177.

The Separation of Belief and Action

Imām Zayn ul-'Ābidīn ﷺ has said:

The most detested people in front of Allah ﷻ are those who accept an Imām and a leader, but do not follow him in regards to his actions.[133]

One of the biggest deficiencies that people commonly face is the separation between what they believe and what they actually do in their lives. Some individuals often speak about how much they like or believe in something, but when you look at their actions, you see that they are not properly acting upon those professed beliefs.

Such people may believe in Allah ﷻ for example, but their actions practically show them as being disbelievers. Another individual may believe in Allah's Justice on the Day of Judgment, but when you look at their morals and ethics, you see that they are practically disbelievers when it comes to that Day.

Such an individual may consider the Prophet of Islam ﷺ as the greatest of the Prophets ﷺ, and Imām 'Alī ﷺ as the greatest of leaders, yet one's actions are not at all in concordance with theirs. In light of this tradition, one should always be careful that their beliefs and actions are in line with one another, for this is the mark of a true believer.

[133] *Tuḥaf al-'Uqūl*, P. 202.

LESSON ONE HUNDRED AND TWENTY-SEVEN

Allah's Punishment

Imām al-Bāqir has said:

Allah has certain punishments which affect the body and the soul, and these include reduced sustenance and feebleness in worship. However, Allah does not punish any of His servants with a more severe punishment than that of hardness of the heart.[134]

Divine punishments are in reality the natural reaction that people earn in place of their negative actions. In some cases, these punishments come in the form of a decrease in one's sustenance, while in other cases, they come in the form of a lack of vitality in worship and one's connection to Allah. However, the most important and dangerous form of punishment is that of hard heartedness. This is when one's heart becomes empty of human emotion and feeling, and where it becomes devoid of all feelings of friendship and social connection.

Such a condition is the root of many great sins and evil actions.

[134] *Tuḥaf al-'Uqūl*, P. 217.

That Which has been Forgotten

Imām aṣ-Ṣādiq has said:

Allah has not created any certainty like death, but (people treat it) as if it were a doubt in which there was never any certainty.[135]

This is a beautiful statement which mentions how unaware people are in regards to the issue of death in spite of its absolute certainty. If people have doubts about anything in their lives, the one thing which is one hundred percent certain is that all of our lives will end and everyone will eventually leave this world. This is a certainty even for those who do not believe in any afterlife or religion. In spite of this, people live their lives as if death does not exist and as if they will live forever.

Since people live their lives in this way, they do not really prepare themselves for what is to come, and they fail to perform good deeds or acts of worship. They do not attempt to purify their souls and strengthen their faith. We should always remember death, and strive to purify our souls so that when the end of our life approaches, we do not leave this world ashamed and embarrassed at what we failed to accomplish and become.

135 *Tuḥaf al-'Uqūl*, P. 271.

The Position of Knowledge and Wisdom

Imām al-Kāẓim ﷺ has said:

Plants grow on soft soil, not on stones. Similarly, knowledge and wisdom sprout only in a humble heart, not in a heart that is filled with arrogance.[136]

The first step in gaining knowledge is to have humility. One must be humble in front of the truth, before one's teacher, and in the presence of anyone who is more knowledgeable. On the opposite side of this, ignorance and arrogance are usually two attributes that come together which prevent one from acquiring true knowledge.

The arrogant are never ready to acknowledge their lack of knowledge. In certain situations, they may even deny something which is true if it does not correspond with their beliefs or actions. In some cases, this denial can even extend into open resistance. In addition, the arrogant are never willing to hear the truth from anyone they consider to be of a lower rank than themselves so they remain submerged in a state of compound ignorance throughout their lives.

[136] *Tuḥaf al-ʿUqūl*, P. 296.

The Heavy Duties of an Imām عليه السلام

Imām ar-Riḍā عليه السلام has said:

An Imām عليه السلام is a trustworthy (representative or vicegerent) of Allah on this earth and amongst His creations. He is Allah's proof among His servants and His deputy in the cities. He is the one who invites (people) toward Allah and is the defender of Allah's sanctum.[137]

[137] *Tuḥaf al-ʿUqūl*, P. 328.

This narration is just a section of the entire tradition which introduces the position of the 12 Divinely-appointed Imāms ﷺ. They are blessed with knowledge from Allah ﷻ, and the rank of immaculateness; and no one except Allah ﷻ can select an individual for such a position. Below are five of the important and heavy responsibilities which the Imāms ﷺ hold:

Imāms ﷺ are the protectors of the Divine revelation; they protect all of the knowledge of Islam.

Imāms ﷺ are the living proof of Allah's religion.

Imāms ﷺ are the guardians of Allah ﷻ and His representatives amongst the people.

Imāms ﷺ are the propagators of the religion, and are the ones who command toward good and forbid against evil.

Imāms ﷺ are the defenders of the Divine sanctuary against the encroachment of enemies.

The Closed Doors will be Opened

Imām al-Jawād has said:

Even if the doors of the heavens and the earth have been closed for someone, if they become God-conscious and observe piety, then Allah will open and make a way out for them.[138]

Sometimes in life, it seems as if all of the doors have been closed on us and everywhere we look, we are faced with difficulties and problems. These trials and circumstances are an opportunity for us to wake up and return back to Allah. Such a return is one that will be constructive and transformative when we connect to Allah through certain means and ask Him for help, He will aid us and send His mercy upon us. Doors will begin to open which we could have never even imagined. In reality, difficulties in life are great opportunities for us to change and come back to Allah, even though they may initially seem like unbearable calamities.

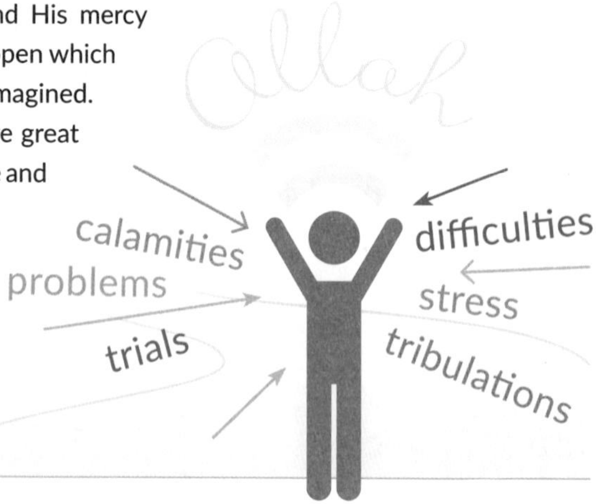

[138] *Nūr al-Abṣār*, P. 150.

Be Careful of People with No Character

Imām al-Hādī ﷺ has said:

Be careful of the evil of people who have no character.[139]

One of the most important things which can prevent evil and corruption is a sense of character and self-respect. Those individuals who have character, even if they are looked down upon by others, will always maintain a standard of good behavior because of the self-respect which they have for themselves. However, if these same people felt that they had no character or self-respect, then they might perform all kinds of evil actions. This is why the 10th Imām ﷺ is saying that we should be careful of such people.

It is for this same reason that one of the important facets of training and educating one's children is through creating self-respect and character for them. When a child senses that they are worthy and other people respect them, this will result in them being careful about what they do both in public and in private, and this will prevent them from partaking in many grave sins and evil actions.

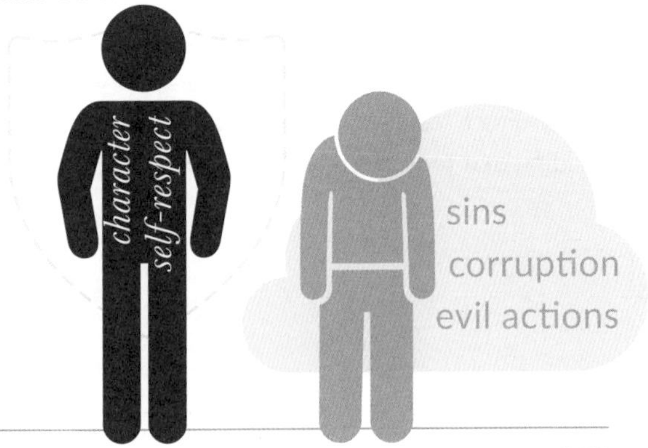

[139] *Tuḥaf al-'Uqūl*, P. 362.

The Greater Struggle (Jihād)

Imām Ḥasan al-ʿAskarī ﷺ has said:

The strongest warrior is one who prevents oneself from sinning.[140]

In Islam, the battle against our negative desires and lusts (which are the main roots of various sins) is called the Greater Struggle (Jihād al-Akbar). Such a fight is considered to be more important than the fight against one's enemies because it is the means to self-purification. Until self-purification takes place, victory over one's enemies is not possible. This is because being defeated by one's enemies is usually the result of personal weaknesses which is due to a lack of character and self-reformation.

The value of this battle is even greater in a society that is filled with corruption, and it will yield much clearer results. The victory of the Prophet ﷺ in the city of Medina was a direct result of the internal battles of the companions and their character building that took place while they were in the city of Mecca.

[140] *Biḥār al-Anwār*, Vol. 78, P. 383.

During the Occultation of Imām al-Mahdī عجل الله تعالى فرجه الشريف

Imām al-Mahdī has said:

Refer to the narrators of our traditions when various events take place during the Greater Occultation.[141]

Human beings can never reach their full potential and purpose of creation without an appropriate leader. For this reason, Allah has never left His servants to themselves without a form of Divine leadership and guidance. This is in the form of our Prophets starting with Prophet Ādam, and through our 12 Imāms right up to Imām al-Mahdī.

When Imām al-Mahdī went into occultation, there was the minor and major occultation. During the minor occultation, the Imām had four deputies whom people could refer to.

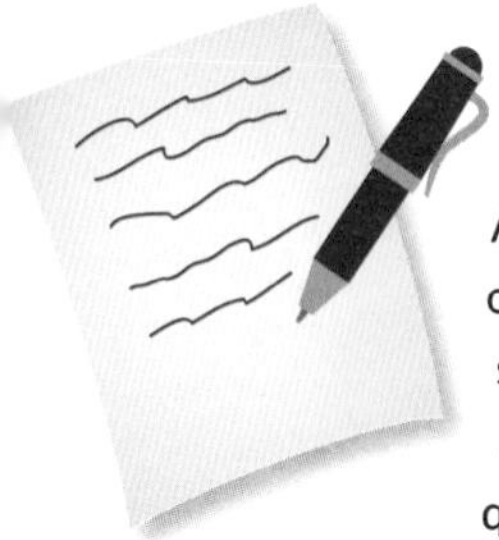

However, the question often asked is who should one refer to for guidance during the major occultation?

According to this tradition, people should refer to the narrators of ḥadīth, meaning the scholars who have certain characteristics such as God-consciousness, justice, obedience toward Allah, resistance of their negative desires, and many other qualifications.

[141] A section of the famous letter from the Imām as taken from various sources.

The Root of All Evil

Prophet Muḥammad ﷺ has said:

Stay away from wine (alcohol) for it is the key to all evils.[142]

Many books and articles have been written on the ill effects of alcohol, and its negative effects have been proven on the nervous system, heart, blood vessels, digestive system, liver, kidneys, and practically all of the organs of the body. Besides these physical negative effects, alcohol is also the cause of many social ills; and the statistics for these are truly astounding. In addition to physical and social ills, there are also spiritual illnesses which arise from alcohol and distance us from our Creator.

These words of the Prophet ﷺ are enough for us to understand that alcohol is the key to many of the evils in this world.

[142] *Nahj al-Faṣāḥah*, P. 1.

LESSON ONE HUNDRED AND THIRTY-SIX

Performing One's Duty is the Greatest Worship

Imām as-Sajjād ﷺ has said:

Whoever performs their necessary duties is the best worshiper among the people.[143]

Worship is neither limited to serving Allah's creation, nor is it limited to only prayers and fasting. Rather, the greatest worship of Allah ﷻ is that in which each person performs one's own necessary duties in life. What kind of worship can be higher and greater than the one through which a society is transformed into a virtual utopia filled with all sorts of blessings and goodness.

What is important to note is that performing one's duties has a wide range of meanings, which includes doing one's duties in terms of the obligatory worship as well. In reality, fulfilling one's responsibilities includes all of the necessary social, cultural, and economic actions which exist. This is in direct contradiction to those who believe that religiosity is achieved by putting aside all worldly duties and simply engaging in acts of ritual worship.

[143] *Wasāʾil ash-Shīʿah*, Vol. 11, P. 206.

The Inhabitants of the Stars

Imām ʿAlī has said:

These stars which are in the sky have cities much like the cities on Earth; each of their cities are connected with a column of light with other cities.[144]

It is extremely selfish for us to imagine that all of the planets and all of the stars in the universe are completely void and empty of inhabitants. The scientists of today have done some research where they have calculated that there should be at least millions, if not hundreds of millions of planets which contain inhabitants in the universe. There is a strong possibility that many of these planets have their own advanced civilizations, some of which may even be more advanced than what is found on Earth. The reason behind this advanced state is due to the fact that life on those planets began many thousands or maybe even millions of years before this Earth. The tradition above is one of the scientific miracles of Imām ʿAlī, who mentioned this over fourteen hundred years ago.

[144] *Safīnat al-Biḥār*, Vol. 3, P. 574.

LESSON ONE HUNDRED AND THIRTY-EIGHT

The Qur'ān and the Law of Gravity

Imām ar-Riḍā is narrated to have said to one of his companions:
'Does not Allah say that the skies are established without any pillar (support structure) that can be seen?'

His companion replied: 'Indeed.'

The Imām then continued:
'Therefore, there exists a pillar which is invisible, that you are not able to see.'[145]

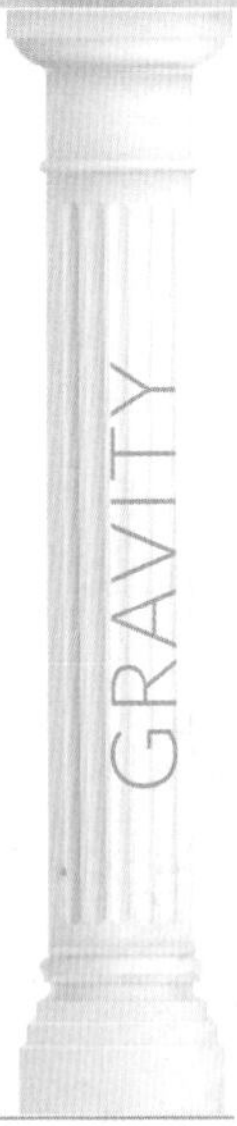

Today, it is firmly established that the Earth and all of the planets travel in their set orbits through the regulation given to them by the phenomenon of gravity. The laws of attraction act much like a great chain which pulls things together, while the law of repulsion pushes things away from one another. This perfect balance allows for all of these immense planets to travel along their own orbits without the least bit of deviation. This is the same invisible pillar which the Qur'ān mentions. What is amazing is that these words were spoken over fourteen centuries ago at a time when the people were completely unaware of such matters—this is another great proof for the truthfulness of the religion of Islam and its message.

[145] *Tafsīr Burhān*, Vol. 3, P. 278.

The Secret of the Mountains

Imām ʿAlī ﷺ has said:

Through means of the mountains, the earth is prevented from shaking and moving.[146]

Today, it has been proven that the moon exerts some kind of influence on the tides and causes their rise and fall each day and night. Due to these effects of the pull of the moon, water levels in an ocean can rise one meter, and in some cases even up to 15 meters in height. In the same way that the moon's pull affects the tides, it also affects the earth's crust as well. The crust is pulled up at least 30 centimeters (almost one foot), after which it contracts back to its normal position.

What keeps the Earth's surface stable and firm is the existence of the mountains whose roots are connected to one another, and which form a network all around the Earth. The presence of these mountains prevents the Earth's crust from shaking and causes it be stable and firm. If the mountains did not exist and the earth continuously was expanding and contracting, then the people would not have been able to live for very long on this planet. This is a reality which the Imāms ﷺ mentioned over fourteen hundred years ago.

[146] *Nahj al-Balāghah*, Sermon 1.

Microscopic Creatures

Imām ar-Riḍā ﷺ has said:

The reason Allah ﷻ is called The Subtle (Al-Laṭīf) is because some of His creations are very small and delicate creatures. These are creatures that we cannot even see and our hands cannot even feel due to their extremely minute size.[147]

This is just a small section of a larger tradition which Fatḥ ibn Yazīd al-Jurjānī has narrated from Imām ar-Riḍā ﷺ. In this tradition, it has been explained that these creatures are so small that our senses cannot perceive them at all. They live amongst the waves of the ocean, the layers of the bark of trees, as well as scattered throughout the deserts and plains.

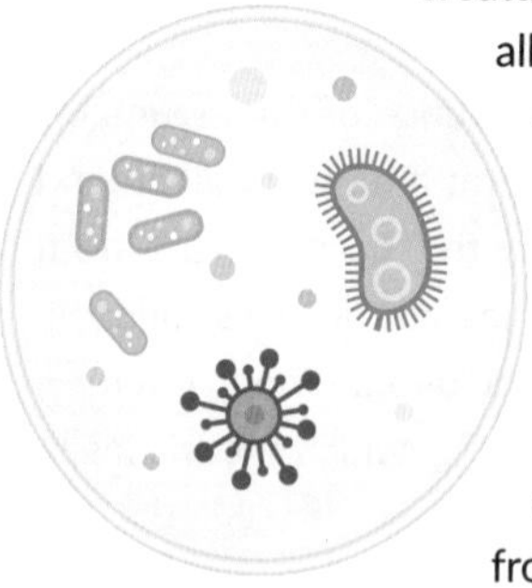

This tradition has been narrated in books that are more than a thousand years old. They were compiled hundreds of years before the birth of Pasteur. This is a clear-cut scientific miracle which has been narrated from Imām ar-Riḍā ﷺ.

[147] *Uṣūl al-Kāfī*, Vol. 1, P. 106; *'Uyūn Akhbār ar-Riḍā*, Vol. 1, P. 127.

They Just Carry the Names of Muslims

Imām ʿAlī ﷺ has said:

A time will come for the people when only the lines will remain of the Qurʾān, and only a name will remain of Islam, and the Masājid of the Muslims will be beautiful in construction but empty of guidance and salvation.[148]

It cannot be said if this prediction has been fulfilled or if it relates to a future era, but what is certain is that some aspects of it are apparent today within our societies. What is stranger yet is that such Muslims are always complaining about a lack of progress, and it is as if they think that only the name of Islam and the written lines of the Qurʾān are enough as a religion. They do not see the Qurʾān as a book of education and human progress, nor do they see Islam as a complete way of life that includes intellectual and scientific developments.

[148] *Nahj al-Balāghah*, Short Saying 369.

The Measure of the Intellect and Ignorance

Imām ʿAlī ﷺ has said:

The tongue is the measure of both the overflowing of ignorance, and the measure of the intellect and wisdom.[149]

The most important gateway into the character and soul of a human being is found in their tongue.

It is the tongue that is the best means of measuring a person's intellect. With just a small movement, the tongue is capable of revealing the deepest motivations and intentions which someone holds inside. It is for this same reason that many of the commandments of Islam revolve around the reformation of the tongue. Indeed, the Immaculate ones ﷺ repeatedly warned about the dangers that can be found in the tongue. It is also obvious that the tongue cannot be reformed unless the spirit and the thoughts of an individual are first reformed. At the same time, it is possible that through much silence and care a person can prevent many of the dangers that often arise from the tongue.

149 *Tuḥaf al-ʿUqūl*, P. 143.

Something Greater than a Blessing!

Imām al-Hādī has said:

The felicity of expressing thanks for a blessing is greater than one's felicity for having received that blessing. This is because blessings are (usually just) a means for the life of this world, whereas thankfulness is an investment both for this world and the next.[150]

Thankfulness is not limited to simply expressing words through one's tongue; it also includes one's actions as well.

Being truly thankful includes utilizing the blessings that one has received in the proper way.

This thankfulness will bring about even further blessings which may make the initial blessing seem small and insignificant in comparison. When blessings are utilized in the way of Allah and for the happiness of His creations, they become a further investment for felicity in both this world and the next. This is because if we look at a blessing itself, it may simply be a material blessing, whereas thankfulness for it extends much higher and is of greater value.

---

[150] *Tuḥaf al-ʿUqūl*, P. 362.

Invigorating the School of Thought of the Ahl al-Bayt عليهم السلام

Imām ar-Riḍā has said:

The heart of anyone who sits in a gathering which invigorates our school of thought will not die on the day when all other hearts will die.[151]

It is apparent from this tradition that one of the duties of the followers of the Ahl al-Bayt is to constantly revitalize their ideology. This includes helping people to understand this school of thought, gain access to its teachings, and taste the essence of the words of the Imāms. These should be gatherings of preparation, self-building, and spirituality, not gatherings of amusement or those in which people simply seek out their material wants and desires, while forgetting their social and spiritual problems. These are gatherings through which the hearts are awakened and brought back to life.

[151] *Mīrāth Imāmān*, P. 443.

LESSON ONE HUNDRED AND FORTY-FIVE

Safeguarding the Secrets

Prophet Muḥammad ﷺ has said:

When someone says something (to another person) and then looks around, their words become a secret and trust (and one must strive to preserve them).[152]

Upholding a trust has various forms in Islam—one of these forms is through preserving the secrets of other people. This is considered to be so important in Islam that revealing the secrets of people is counted as one of the greater sins. It is not even necessary for an individual to mention that what they are telling you should be kept a secret; it is enough for them to simply look around in a certain manner as if being careful of those who are within range. This suffices for such words to be considered a secret and it becomes obligatory for one to safeguard these entrusted things.

Revealing the secrets of people is counted as one of the greater sins.

[152] *Nahj al-Faṣāḥah*, P. 38.

LESSON ONE HUNDRED AND FORTY-SIX

Signs of True Faith

Prophet Muḥammad ﷺ has said:

If your good actions make you happy and your bad actions make you sad, then you are a believing individual.[153]

Islam has mentioned that everyone is born with a pure inner nature—this includes an intrinsic faith in Allah ﷻ and a love of all that is good. As time passes, it is possible for sins to gradually affect the soul of an individual and influence it in such a way where it is completely transformed from this original state. In spite of this, as long as someone loves what is good and hates what is bad, it is clear that the spirit of faith and one's pure inner nature is still present and healthy within them.

It is truly the wretched people who do not become sad at their evil actions, and a step beyond this is when they actually become happy.

[153] *Nahj al-Faṣāḥah*, P. 41.

The First Condition of Every Action

Imām ʿAlī ﷺ has said:

There is no action or work except that you need awareness, comprehension, and understanding in its performance.[154]

If we reflect on the words 'There is no action or work...' then we will become familiar with the extent of the Islamic program for life. The religion of Islam is not only a program for worship and supplication, or only a belief system without any practical applications.

Islam is in reality a program for the entirety of our lives, and this includes both personal issues, as well as social.

This program extends to every action that we perform. The first step toward enacting this program is awareness and understanding the reality of things; without understanding ourselves and the reality around us properly, all of our actions and efforts will be without a proper effect, or at least they will be lessened in their effectiveness.

[154] *Safīnat al-Biḥār*, Vol. 1, P. 15.

LESSON ONE HUNDRED AND FORTY-EIGHT

The Importance of Guests

Prophet Muḥammad ﷺ has said:

Whenever Allah ﷻ wishes goodness and felicity for someone, He gives them a gift.

He was asked: "What gift does He give?" The Prophet ﷺ replied: "Guests!"[155]

Without a doubt, guests are a great gift from the Divine who possess value and honor. Unfortunately, in today's materialistically oriented world, the custom of serving guests has seemingly lost its value. When we look at many countries, we find that the idea of having guests come over is not like what it used to be in time's past. In some cases, they are even seen as an annoyance and bother, and it is becoming rare for people to invite others to their home, or to accept invitations unless there is a type of economic or political (materialistically oriented) motivation involved. Yet, if we look at much of the Muslim world or within specific religious families, we will see that guests are greatly honored, even if they are not well-known to the host family.

We should always keep in mind that guests are a gift from Allah ﷻ, and we should treat and honor them accordingly.

---

[155] *Biḥār al-Anwār*, Vol. 15, P. 241.

Respect and Love

Imām aṣ-Ṣādiq has said:

One who does not respect the elders and is not affectionate toward the young is not from among us.[156]

Human society is much like a caravan that is always in motion; children are born and soon grow up, while the adults age and become older, eventually passing away. No one amongst these travelers can bypass this natural process. In this caravan, the elders usually have more experience and wisdom due to the lives that they have lived. If they lived their lives properly, then they are also the source of much good in this world. Due to this reason, they are to be respected and honored by those who are younger than them. At the same time, the youth are newer to this world and they are just starting their lives, so they must be loved and treated with complete care and consideration. This is the proper way that the youth and the elders are to be treated in a balanced and caring society.

[156] *Uṣūl al-Kāfī*, Vol. 3, P. 253.

LESSON ONE HUNDRED AND FIFTY

Invest in Yourself

Imām 'Alī ﷺ has said:

What you send ahead of yourselves will be saved for you, and what you delay will end up benefitting others (however its responsibility will remain with you).[157]

It appears that the desire of people to accumulate wealth has increased during modern times to much higher levels than before. Unfortunately, such people accumulate wealth without considering what their main goals in life are, and at some point, it really does seem like an illogical and even insane thing to do. Such individuals get so involved in the accumulation of wealth that they sometimes lose sight of whether they are making that money through lawful or unlawful means. Do such people even think about the fact that they will not be able to take their wealth with them when they leave this world, nor will they be able to spend all of it during the span of their lives? At some point, they will have to leave all of their wealth behind and the only thing that will remain with them will be the responsibility of that wealth.

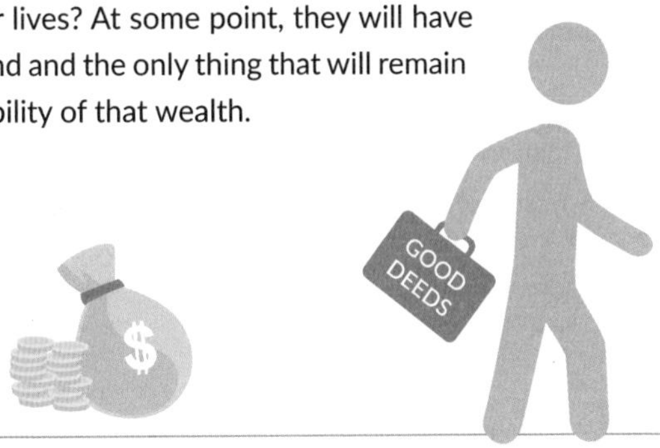

[157] *Nahj al-Balāghah*; *Ghurar al-Ḥikam*, P. 104.

Glossary of Terms

Ahl al-Bayt ﷺ**:** Literally means "People of the House." Designation in Islam for select family members of Prophet Muḥammad ﷺ, particularly his daughter Lady Fāṭimah az-Zahrā' ﷺ, her husband Imām 'Alī ﷺ, their sons Imām Ḥasan ﷺ and Imām Ḥusayn ﷺ, and the nine specific descendants from the progeny of Imām Ḥusayn ﷺ.

Ahl as-Sunnah: The largest branch of Islam that was formed after the death of Prophet Muḥammad ﷺ. They do not believe in the Divine successor-ship of Imām 'Alī ﷺ, and the Imāms ﷺ who came after him, and instead follow the teaching of the caliphs. They are also referred to as the Sunnīs.

Alḥamdulillāh: All praise is for Allah ﷻ (God).

Allah ﷻ**:** The Arabic term for God, a culmination of all of His Names and Titles.

Al-Laṭīf: The Subtle; a Name of Allah ﷻ.

'Āshūrā': The tenth day of Muḥarram (the first month of the Islamic calendar), and the day when the Battle of Karbalā' took place in which Imām Ḥusayn ﷺ and his family, companions, and close friends were martyred.

Bismillāhir Raḥmānir Raḥīm: (I begin) In the Name of Allah, the All-Kind (or All-Beneficent), the All-Merciful (or All-Compassionate).

Dhāt: Essence.

Du'ā': Supplication; a deep connection and communication between an individual and Allah ﷻ.

Farūq: One who discerns and distinguishes between truth and falsehood.

Ghayrah: A sense of loyalty and protectiveness over one's religion and family.

Ghayūr: An individual who has a protective sense toward one's religion, one's people, and one's family.

Ḥadīth: A tradition or narration from Prophet Muḥammad ﷺ or the 12 Imāms ﷺ that include sayings and actions.

Ḥajj: A pilgrimage to Mecca performed in the 12th Islamic month of Dhūl Ḥijjah that is obligatory upon every Muslim once in a person's lifetime when certain conditions are met. It is one of the ten Furū' ad-Dīn (Branches of the Religion).

Ḥalāl: Something lawful; permissible; allowed.

Ḥarām: Something forbidden; not allowed. Engaging in this action will entail a punishment.

Imām: Literally means 'a leader,' and can refer to a local community religious leader; or the prayer leader of an Islamic center. However, its most specific usage is in terms of the 12 Divinely-appointed guides (Imāms ﷺ) chosen by Allah ﷻ.

Inshā'Allāh: God-willing.

Jihād al-Akbar: The Greater Struggle; the battle against our negative desires and lusts.

Marḥūmīn: Literally means 'those who are in the mercy (of Allah ﷻ);' refers to those who have passed away.

Masājid: (singular is Masjid) Mosques.

Ma'ṣūmīn: These are the 14 Immaculate beings who are inerrant (free of all sins, flaws, and impurities) who never committed any sins in their entire lives—they include Prophet Muḥammad ﷺ, Lady Fāṭimah az-Zahrā' ﷺ, and the 12 Imāms ﷺ beginning with Imām 'Alī ﷺ up to Imām al-Mahdī ﷺ.

Mujāhidīn: Those who struggle (do jihād) in the way of Allah ﷻ; Warriors.

Qur'ān: The final of the Books or Scriptures sent by Allah ﷻ to the Prophets ﷺ for the guidance of humanity; this book was sent to Prophet Muḥammad ﷺ and is the holy Book of the Muslims.

Ribā: Literally means 'usury' or 'exorbitant amounts of interest' charged to an individual who seeks to borrow money (or any commodity). In Islam the concept of ribā is forbidden.

Ṣabr: Literally means 'patience and fortitude,' it is a noble ethical trait related to having patience in the face of difficulties; when we are performing our responsibilities; and to be steadfast against sinning. Ṣabr does not mean to sit back and not do anything when trials come our way, but rather to endeavor to pull through them to the best of our ability.

Ṣalāh: Literally means 'prayers,' and in Islamic terminology, this word refers to the specific method of prayer that has been legislated by Allah. It can refer to the five daily prayers that Muslims perform, such as Ṣalāt al-Fajr, Ṣalāt al-Maghrib, etc.; or any of the other prayers such as: Ṣalāt al-Jumu'ah; Ṣalāt al-Āyāt, etc.

Salāmun 'alaykum: Islamic greeting that translates as: Peace be upon you.

Shayṭān: (Satan)—Literally means 'the devil,' generally used to speak about the devilish individuals from humanity and jinn who seek to create mischief and misguide people from the path of Allah. It is also used to speak specifically about the jinn known as 'Iblīs'—the prime instigator who was removed from the Kingdom of the mercy of Allah due to his willful disregard of the commands of Allah and his disobedience to Him.

Shī'ah: Literally means 'a follower,' however when used in Islamic terminology, it refers to the followers of the first Imām, 'Alī ibn Abī Ṭālib. The Shī'ahs believe that Allah designated Imām 'Alī to succeed Prophet Muḥammad after his death, and after him, this leadership transferred to his son, Imām Ḥasan, then to Imām Ḥusayn, to the select line of nine Imāms, ending with Imām al-Mahdī who is still alive.

Ṣiddīq: A truthful individual.

Subḥanallāh: All glory and praise belongs to Allah.

Sunnah: The practice of the Prophet or Imāms.

Sūrah al-Fātiḥah: The first chapter (sūrah) of the Qur'ān, which is commonly recited and sent as a gift of prayer for the deceased; it is also recited in every prayer (ṣalāh).

Tawfīq: Divine blessings from Allah that gives a person the opportunity and ability to thrive toward success.

'Ulamā': Muslim scholars recognized as having specialist knowledge of Islamic sacred law and theology.

Wuḍū': The ritual process of ablution by which a Muslim prepares oneself for many acts of worship such as praying, performing the rituals of Ḥajj or 'Umrah, touching the script of the Qur'ān in Arabic, or the Name of Allah in any language, and certain other things. Without this special ablution, these things will not be valid and/or cannot be performed.

Zāhid: Ascetic; a person who is not attached to worldly things.

Zakāh: One of the obligatory forms of Islamic taxation. Based on numerous verses of the Qur'ān and traditions from the Immaculate ones, the scholars of Islamic Jurisprudence highlight the various items upon which zakāh is obligatory, and the quantity that must be paid.

The 12 Imāms ﷿*

1. Imām ʿAlī ﷿
2. Imām Ḥasan ﷿
3. Imām Ḥusayn ﷿
4. Imām ʿAlī as-Sajjād (Zayn al-ʿĀbidīn) ﷿
5. Imām Muḥammad al-Bāqir ﷿
6. Imām Jaʿfar aṣ-Ṣādiq ﷿
7. Imām Mūsā al-Kāẓim ﷿
8. Imām ʿAlī ar-Riḍā ﷿
9. Imām Muḥammad at-Taqī al-Jawād ﷿
10. Imām ʿAlī al-Hādī an-Naqī ﷿
11. Imām Ḥasan al-ʿAskarī ﷿
12. Imām Muḥammad al-Mahdī عجل الله تعالى فرجه الشريف

* The 12 leaders as mentioned by Prophet Muḥammad ﷺ in Lesson 119, on P. 154.

Index

S

T

U

W

About the Board ʿĀlim

Moulana Nabi R. Mir (Abidi) is a scholar, an educator, a father, and an enthusiast for creating educational infrastructure and Islamic resources for the benefit of the global community. Always wanting to think 'outside of the box' by supporting the creation of innovative materials to engage young readers to pick up Islamic books, interact with Qur'ānic games, learn from the Steps to Perfection Curriculum, and begin their life-long journey of holistic education.

Being a dedicated student and graduate of *Darse Khārij* from the *Ḥawzah* (the Highest Level of Islamic Studies in the Seminary), Moulana Abidi knows the value of Islamic education. Also, having grown up in India, and now residing in the United States, he has had the honor of traveling to various communities and meeting many community leaders. He values the importance of collaboration and working together to optimize potentials, and to create open source platforms so that information and resources are available and accessible to everyone around the world.

You, dear reader, are now part of the Al-Kisa family.
Share the word, and join the mission.